Remembering Carlow

Maria O'Rourke

Hardback edition

First published 2024 by Marble City Publishing

ISBN-10 1-908943-97-1

ISBN-13 978-1-908943-97-2

Cover art – painting of the Dublin Road by Colette Keenan

Cover design – Jack O'Flaherty

Dedication

For my mother, Margaret O'Rourke, and all the people
who shared their memories of Carlow, without whom this
book would not have been possible.

Contents

Court House, Carlow.

Acknowledgements

I would like to acknowledge all those whose conversations with
me allowed this book to develop into a valuable record of the
social history of Carlow town.

Thanks also to Michael Purcell, The Lawrence Collection and The Carlow
Nationalist for allowing photographs to be used.

I am also grateful to Christopher, John and Deirdre
in Carlow library for their help.

Finally, to the following patrons:
Swan's Electrical, Bramley's, Nursery Rhymes, Jennings Opticians,
Thomas M. Byrne and Healy's Undertakers for their generous support.

Section 1

'Living Over the Shop'

Introduction to 'Living Over the Shop'

Older Carlovians will remember a time when Tullow Street and Dublin Street were the heart of Carlow. Both sides of the streets were lined with small and medium sized shops which were family owned and run. Every shop had its loyal customers and its fair share of characters. These were places we visited when we went 'downtown' – the grocery stores, hardwares, furniture shops, drapers, fishmongers. This section revisits a time when the shops were all clustered in just a few narrow streets, where a shilling a week could be paid to secure an item and trust between shopkeeper and customer was everything.

To put this series of articles together, I interviewed the surviving members of families who ran businesses for over fifty years in Carlow town, exploring how they came to set up in business, what their memories are and what became of the family enterprise in time. I learned about characters many will remember, about celebrations and disasters that befell them, getting a unique view of what life was like on the other side of the counter and what it was like to 'live over the shop' in a town that has changed beyond recognition.

Some of these businesses have survived the arrival of chain stores and supermarkets. Others simply changed hands or went out of business altogether. Ireland and Carlow are very different places than they were fifty years ago, and my goal was to capture what we've lost so that it will never be forgotten. I loved chatting with all the contributors and hearing the unique stories of where their families hailed from and how they established their family businesses. The following articles may surprise and delight you. I hope they bring back happy memories and prompt people to talk about the past, particularly to young people. As Theodore Roosevelt said, 'The more you know about the past, the better prepared you are for the future.'

'Good with the Bad Eye!'

Many people from Carlow and the surrounding areas will remember a hardware store which was situated at 140 Tullow Street, with the title W.P. Good over the door. Speaking to Keith Good, I learned the story of how his grandfather, William Patterson Good, came to Carlow in 1911, having served his time in the drapery trade all over Ireland and finally in Fordes of Carlow (later to become Haddens). He purchased number 9 Dublin Street originally, which had formerly belonged to John and William Ross, who traded as 'boot and shoemakers, warehouses and dealers.' This premises was known as The White House and was next to the Royal Hotel and Gurley's Lane.

William developed this business to include hardware and bicycle repairs. Business was going well, so when 140 Tullow Street came up for sale in 1919, he purchased it as a going concern. It had previously belonged to David Henry and was a substantial premises with good overhead accommodation. William was a man with a short temper and because of a cast in his eye, he was known locally as 'Good with the bad eye!' He was clearly a man with a good eye for business though, and an imaginative, creative mind as can be seen by studying his advertisements in the local paper, one of which boldly stated '1000 Men Wanted' before explaining that they were wanted to buy his suits, overcoats, riding breeches etc. The Dublin Street premises was sold in 1924 and William focused his business interests on Tullow Street. After the death of his first wife, he married Sarah Bagnall from Mayo in 1920. In 1921 Keith's father, George William Good, was born.

'Good with the bad eye!' William Patterson Good 1883 – 1954

Over the next thirty years, William Good developed his hardware business until his sudden death in 1954 at home. He collapsed in the dining room at the rear of the premises and died instantly. By this time, his only son, George, was 33 years old and already working in the business for many years. George expanded the business further to include a farm machinery business in Barrack Street which remained open until 1972.

At this time in Carlow, Thursday was a 'closed day.' That was the day when shopkeepers collected stock from wholesalers in Dublin. Deliveries from Dublin were often transported by goods train to the railway store at Carlow Station, before being sorted and delivered by CIE horse and wagon.

Keith remembers, 'The fun bit was in persuading the horse to reverse the four-wheel wagon to turn in our narrow yard!'

Storage sheds surrounded the yard to the rear of the shop and a dry cellar was used for storage of plumbing fittings, nuts and bolts of every kind, marley floor tiles, wall tiles etc. George Good spent much of his working time in the office surrounded by a 'Players' fog. According to Keith he smoked non-stop, although he gave it up after a heart-attack in 1969. The staff were unionised, and George always adhered to nationally agreed rates set by the *Irish Union of Distributive Workers and Clerks*. Although Keith remembers that every time a wage increase was notified by post, George's muttering would escalate to new heights. He constantly worried that the business would become unviable and was never relaxed except when fishing.

Valuable members of staff over the years were Maura Forbes, who ran the office, assisted by Hazel Graham (Wynne) followed by Theresa Carey and Mary Hennessy. There was Barney O'Brien, Tom Byrne, Oliver Pender, Bernie Walsh, Mary Fitzgibbon, John Fitzpatrick as well as Tony Kirwan who drove the Transit delivery pick-up. In 1965, the oil store at the back of the premises went on fire and was damaged. However, George turned this to his advantage when, with the insurance money, he repaired the shed, sold off the fire-damaged stock, including stock he had bought in specially from Dublin suppliers and brought in by the vanload!

Keith ended up in the business accidentally as he had begun to train as an estate agent in Dublin, at his father's request, but hadn't liked it. He joined the family at 140 Tullow Street in 1969, which coincided with his father's heart attack. He began to help out and never left! In 1973, George appointed Keith as a director of the company. Keith is almost embarrassed by what ensued. His parents wondered what the staff should now address him as and settled on 'Mr. Keith.' Times have certainly changed!

Keith married his wife Ann Corcoran in 1972, proving that he was not a traditionalist. Since Ann was a Catholic, theirs was what was known as a 'mixed marriage.' Ann would have had to promise to bring the children up as Catholics if they were to marry in the Catholic church. Neither of them was prepared to do this and the couple married quietly in the Methodist Church on the Athy Road, having their wedding breakfast in the Leinster Arms Hotel in Athy. They then honeymooned in the family caravan in Enniscrone, County Sligo. The couple went on to have four beautiful daughters.

In 1977, Good's acquired Goughs shop next door at 139, which had been closed for some years, on the condition that Mr. George Gough could remain in residence upstairs for his lifetime. When he died three years later, Keith met with George's surviving sister in Dublin to arrange for the removal of his furniture and effects. A front window was taken out and a stairway was fitted to a lorry below and all the furniture was carried out to the street.

By now Good's had extended their shop and knocked down the adjoining wall to make a huge showroom. However, the overheads of such a large shop and extra staff meant that the business was not thriving. In 1981, George was approached by Thomas Kehoe, auctioneer, enquiring if he might be interested in leasing part of the premises to a large British company. It was a difficult decision, but the offer was accepted, the dividing wall built up again and Saxone Shoes moved in next door.

George was slowing down at this time and was greatly saddened by the death of his long-term friend, Harry Sutton of Suttons Supermarket, in 1987. In 1988, he retired from the business and Keith and Ann bought his shareholding, forming a trading company called 'Keith and Ann Good' and running a successful wallpaper and paint business until 1996, when Thomas Kehoe again came along with another offer they couldn't refuse from the chain 'Eurogiant' and Good's was no more.

Keith and Ann have never regretted the decision to step back from business and are enjoying retirement surrounded by their family and a plethora of interesting memories.

Good's Shop on Tullow Street

Hard Work and Loyal Service

A popular Carlow man whose family has been in business in the town since the 1940s, is Seán Swan, owner of Swans Expert electrical shop in the Strawhall Industrial Estate. Seán originally hails from number 5 Coalmarket, and grew up in the shadow of Carlow Castle. His story and that of his family is an interesting one, steeped in hard work and serving the community.

Seán's grandfather was steward of a farm in Ballickmoyler and a founder member of the Irish Volunteers there in 1914. His son, John, Seán's father, became an adjutant in the Old IRA, E Company, Laois Brigade, and was imprisoned twice by the British. He was buried with full military honours in 1975. In the 1930s, times were difficult for farmers as there was an embargo on trade with Britain. For this reason, John decided to sell the farm and bought a grocery shop in Carlow, formerly owned by a Mrs. Doran, where he and his wife reared their three children, Sheila, Pat and Seán. Although a small shop, it was well supported, especially by the country people who remembered John from his farming days.

At that time Coalmarket, which is situated between Castle Street and Castle Hill, was a thriving business community, despite being prone to flooding. There were two pubs, Murphys and O'Neills, Broughan's hardware and petrol pumps, Purcells greengrocers, Shanaghys ice-cream parlour and Farrells. Swan's, like most of the businesses at the time, operated a credit system and, since many of their customers were farmers, it wasn't unusual to have to wait for the bill to be settled when the harvest came in. Seán remembers when Buggy's Buses ran a bus from Castlecomer to Carlow once a week, taking in Killeshin and Rossmore. People would leave in their list of 'messages' and while they were doing other business in town, Swan's would fulfil their orders and deliver boxes bearing the customer's name to the empty bus which was parked in Haymarket. They were honest days and the goods would be intact when the shoppers returned.

Swan's of Coalmarket with the flood waters in front

As a child and teenager, Seán helped out in the shop. Tea had to be weighed into quarter and half pound bags from a large, aluminium foil-covered chest. Sugar from Suttons Wholesale arrived in hundredweight bags and had to be weighed into 2lb, 7lb and 14lb bags. In the 1950s butter was scarce, and butter known as 'Black Swan' butter arrived from Australia in a box shaped like a pyramid. There was also 'bully beef' which came from Argentina. Some farming people would barter for their shopping, bringing in eggs or 'country butter' in exchange for 'the messages.' For helping out, Seán was given pocket money each week, something a lot of his friends didn't have. The seeds of business acumen were clearly already sown when Seán, having finished reading his weekly comic, rented it to others for thruppence the first week, then tuppence the next and finally a penny on the third week!

On a Sunday evening, young men cycled in from the country areas to go to the cinema in town. Their bikes were parked at the Garda barracks in Tullow Street as there were bars to lock bikes to there. However, they left their coats, lamps and pumps to be minded in Swan's. After the cinema, Seán's father would have the results of all the GAA matches ready and would sit discussing games and news with the men till the small hours. When Éire Óg were involved in a match, John would treat the team to a drink and a bun. Seán continues this tradition in a different way to this day, being Éire Óg's sponsor since 1992 – the longest continual sponsorship in the country.

In the early 1970s, Seán's parents decided to retire and the shop passed to his brother, Pat. Many will remember his endearing, warm personality. Full of enthusiasm and ideas, Pat bought number 6 Coalmarket and turned the two premises into 'Swan's Foodmarket,' famed for its cooked chickens on a Sunday morning – a new phenomenon for Carlow. Pat was famous for his catchy window signs, e.g. under the price of fish he would write 'This is no cod!' And when Albert Goubé opened a massive supermarket on the Tullow Road, trading as 'Three Guys,' Pat wrote 'It will take more than three guys to beat this one guy!' Unfortunately, the onset of multiple supermarket chains did eventually signal the end for Swans in the grocery trade, but their contribution has not been forgotten.

Having left school, Seán worked for Corcoran's wholesale business where he says he learned valuable skills. When that business closed in 1966, he bought a van and sourced grocery and other items to supply small shops throughout the region. This business was so successful that by 1980 he had seven vans on the road, serving the entire Southeast. While still conducting this business, Seán opened an electrical shop beside his brother, Pat, in number 7 in 1976. His wife, Patricia, grew the business through the 1980s and in 1996 they moved the business to Tullow Street. In 2000, an even bigger premises was needed and Seán opened in Strawhall Industrial Estate, which was extended again in 2008.

Seán Swan

Seán Swan's business has been part of the 'Expert' group of electrical stores for the past 20 years, where he also serves as a Board member. He firmly believes in businesses working together. Asked the secret of his business success, he puts it down to hard work, taking the rough with the smooth and being confident when dealing with financial institutions. When he was only twelve years old one of his group of friends asked the others what they would like to be when they were grown up. While the others all answered with jobs such as banking, farming or the pub trade, Seán said he wanted to be an entrepreneur – a word his friends had to look up in the dictionary! That was more than an idle boast and the twin spirits of community service and business savvy, passed down from his parents, have served Carlow well.

From King William to 'Whistling John'

Speaking with Beatrice Byrne (nee Lambert), whose family has run a business in Dublin Street Carlow since 1964, I heard the story of 'Lamberts Coffee House,' which occupies numbers 16 and 17 Dublin Street, Carlow and dates back to the 17th Century at least. The popular coffee shop is now in the hands of Beatrice's son, Brian Byrne, and his wife, Zoe, who continue the family tradition to this day.

In the 17th Century, numbers 16 and 17 Dublin Street were one building, The Globe Inn, which was one of the oldest inns in Carlow Town, and was owned by William and Ruth Watson. It was extended in 1699 which was marked by a plaque on the wall which still exists, bearing the inscription WIR 1699. It is said that King William lodged in The Globe Inn and wrote one of his dispatches there after the Battle of the Boyne.

It isn't certain when The Globe Inn closed or when it was divided into two premises, but we know that since 1870 it belonged to a John Core who ran an orchard in the long back garden. Known as 'The Apple Man' and 'Whistling John,' legend has it that he insisted the boys who worked for him whistled constantly. His theory was that if they were whistling, they couldn't be eating apples.

Beatrice's father, John Joe Lambert, bought the premises in 1964 from Miss McElwee. A condition of the sale was that the McElwee name had to be left over the door until the last of the family died. This was honoured until Miss McElwee's brother, who lived in Burrin Street, died some years later. John Joe, a painter and decorator by trade, had some retail experience, since

15

he had been reared by an aunt who owned a small shop on Staplestown Road. The plan was that John Joe would continue his painting business, which also involved signwriting and making brass breastplates for coffins, while Bridie would run the shop. Beatrice remembers how dark the premises was when the family was brought to see it and it took some time before it was ready to be occupied.

By this time three of Beatrice's older siblings had already left home, so John Joe, his wife Bridie, Julie, JJ, Beatrice and Leo moved into number 16 while number 17 was Cunninghams barber shop, run by Mr. Cunningham and his daughter, Rita. The family entrance was in Brown Street while the newsagents and small grocery shop faced Dublin Street. The first employee, Mary Scully, was a teenager when she started working in Lamberts and stayed her entire working life, greeting people and selling newspapers in her friendly, open manner. Mary cycled to work from Ballickmoyler every day and was a much loved part of the fabric of Carlow town.

Many people wonder why there are short, granite posts at the side of Lamberts shop on Brown Street. Beatrice explained that beside these posts there was a gate opening onto a cobbled pathway which led behind all the premises as far as the Irishman's Bar. The posts were to assist people getting on and off their horses when entering this narrow lane. In an inside window of Lamberts lies another monument to the past, in the form of an old weighing scales which was used to weigh sweets for countless Carlow children and adults over the years.

While they lived at home, John Joe expected all his children to help out with the early morning delivery of newspapers. Perhaps this is how Beatrice turned out to be such a champion runner, winning her first Irish championship aged just 11, and in 1970 winning the Irish Under 13, 15 and 17 cross-country championships with John Joe as her trainer. He was very involved in the St.

Laurence O'Toole's Running Club and encouraged many local runners to get involved in the sport.

Lamberts was always a place of conversation and debate. Beatrice's mother, Bridie, sat on a stool outside the counter and chatted with everyone, with people coming to her for advice and to discuss the news. Beatrice remembers an early morning customer, neighbour PaJoe Tierney, would stand with his hands behind his back, declaring, 'Get the name of an early riser and you can stay in bed all day!' The shop opened at 7.30 each morning and stayed open until 7pm. Other regulars who took part in the ongoing daily conversation were Cran Hogan and Paddy Kelly from Ballymahon Terrace.

Photo of Brown Street showing the horse posts at the side of Lamberts.
Credit IGP Carlow

A terrible sadness visited Lamberts when the youngest member of the family, Leo, died aged just 22, from an aggressive form of cancer. Beatrice remembers it having a huge effect on her parents and casting a sadness over the whole family and locality. When John Joe died aged seventy, the shop was taken over by Beatrice and her husband, John Byrne. Together they expanded the business and rejoined the two premises as one again. They began to sell a wider variety of confectionary and magazines, comics and groceries. Sadness again visited in 2013, when John died on his 60th birthday to the inexpressible grief of his family.

These days, Lamberts has been given a whole new lease of life since being handed over to Beatrice's son, Brian, his wife, Zoe, and family. Together they have transformed the premises into a chic coffee shop, Lamberts Coffee House, beloved of Carlow people, young and old. During the legal handover, Beatrice discovered a surprise that delighted her son, Brian. Fishing rights were attached to the house for years and still apply to this day. A bonus! Brian and Zoe did extensive renovations to the premises during the Covid pandemic and what has emerged is a business and meeting place which I'm sure would make John Joe and Bridie very proud.

John Joe and Bridie Lambert outside their newsagents

From Russia to Carlow

A fascinating tale of fortitude unfolded when I spoke with Peter Robinson whose father, Abe (Abraham), and grandfather, Philip (Jacob), ran a furniture shop in Burrin Street, Carlow. Their shop was a first stop for newly married couples for almost a century. Peter, who is still in the retail trade with his wife, Debbie (Nursery Rhymes), collaborated with his siblings – twin brother John and sister, Phillipa, to compile memories of their family business which was a feature of Carlow life for many years.

Jacob Robinson, a Jewish man, arrived in Ireland in the late 19th Century, having fled the pogroms of Russia, when Jewish people had to flee for their lives. His family had first moved to England. Having heard that he could make a living in Ireland as a pedlar, he began roaming from town to town, buying and selling whatever he could. When he had secured enough to settle down, he chose Carlow as there was a small Jewish community there and the property was more affordable than in the cities.

Jacob's Yiddish name was Yakov, but he was advised to adopt a more English sounding name and chose Philip – although he was unsure as to whether that was spelled with a P or an F, so the name he chose to put over the shop was PF Robinson and Sons. The P was later dropped. Along with his wife, Fanny, and their three eldest children, Rose, Ben and Miriam, they settled in Burrin Street where four more children were born, Aaron (Harry), Abraham (Abe), Esther and Henry. All the boys worked in the furniture store after school before joining the family business full-time once their schooling was complete. Abe told his children stories of going to school in College Street in his bare feet and that he left school at fifteen.

The business was a success and gradually grew. Many new housing estates were springing up around Carlow, all needing affordable furniture. When Jacob died in 1959, his sons Abe and Henry took over the business, extending and remodelling it in 1969. Abe specialised in buying and selling antique furniture, although Peter adds that unfortunately he didn't always know the true value of it and sometimes sold items at a loss. He was closely monitored by antique dealers looking for a bargain.

Henry and Abe Robinson

Abe and Henry were known to be very generous businessmen. They would regularly include an extra chair or table as a gift to newlyweds. The affordable floor covering of the time was linoleum or 'lino' and customers would often come into the shop with a piece of string saying they wanted 'this much lino!' Abe had married Adele Cuckle, an English woman from a Jewish family who was sixteen years his junior, in 1954 and a new generation of Robinsons began with the birth of Phillipa and twins, Peter and John. Peter remembers that their childhood summers were spent climbing on rolls of carpet and playing at the back of the shop. There always seemed to be a new corner to discover.

The success of the business was largely down to the implementation of a hire purchase scheme, which enabled many people to furnish a house with a small down payment followed by affordable weekly payments. On Monday mornings one of the Robinsons would call, door to door, collecting the weekly payments. There was a yellow card, which was updated every week. Abe's motto was 'It doesn't matter what you pay, as long as you pay something.' Most houses in Carlow were furnished in this way.

Deliveries over the years were done by Billy Hickey, followed by Paddy Mullins, both loyal employees who served the business for a long time. They were skilled at loading three houses' worth of furniture into a small van! Jim Galway was another driver who, on his first delivery to Dublin, was missing for hours and reported that he had to drive around a roundabout seven times to find his way off! Another valued member of staff was Breda O'Connor who looked after the office and always had a kind word for customers. The phone number was Carlow 52 and it never stopped ringing!

The shop in Burrin Street was situated right beside the river, so flooding was a constant threat. On several occasions, the shop was flooded, with much of the stock being ruined. Unfortunately, the proximity to water didn't stop the premises being engulfed in fire in 1976. The Robinson family were just having their breakfast, it was close to 9am and somebody called to the door and said, 'Your shop is on fire.' Peter says it was the only time in his life he saw his father cry. Significant fire and water damage was caused, and it took a few months before the business reopened. However, it's an ill wind! Peter recalls that in the 'fire damaged' sale, Robinsons managed to sell items that had been in stock for years which nobody had wanted before.

Robinsons on fire in 1976

When Abe Robinson died in 1982, Peter, who had worked there since he left school, took over his role in the business, partnered by his Uncle Henry. In his obituary, Abe was remembered as a man who furnished many homes of newly married couples at little or no cost to them. He and his wife were charitable and quietly helped many people in need. The young Peter and Henry worked together until Henry's death in 1999. At this point, large wholesale stores were beginning to dominate the market and business became difficult. Peter hoped to redevelop the site, but planning permission was refused and, in the year 2000, he made the difficult decision to close the doors.

Robinsons also ran other successful businesses in Carlow and beyond over the years. At different times they had five betting offices in the region, as well as a jewellery shop in Dublin Street. Peter remembers once having to repossess an engagement ring that hadn't been paid for. The ring came back, but whether the marriage survived is a mystery!

Although Peter is very happily still working in the retail trade, he says he has no wish for any of his four daughters to continue it. They are all building careers of their own, so the Robinson contribution to the business life of Carlow will stop with him. It will be gone, but not forgotten as their family has played an important role in the lives of so many people for generations.

Cycles, Sales and Service

Walter Coleman hails from a family business which has served the people of Carlow since 1859. Sadly, this era has come to an end with the retirement of Walter in early 2024, but the memory of his family's contribution to the life of the town will live on for many years.

Walter's family story begins with his great-grandfather, Benjamin, who opened a paint and glazier shop at 19 Dublin Street, a building occupied by the family business until 2005. In 1903, he acquired a premises in Charlotte Street which had been the Methodist Hall for the previous hundred years. (Allegedly the Methodists moved because of the noxious smell coming from the four slaughterhouses in the vicinity at the time.) It was converted to a garage for maintaining cars and was one of the first workshops in the country. At that time all car parts came as standard sizes and had to be customised to fit individual cars, a skill developed by Benjamin and his son, Alfred.

Benjamin's garage was in operation when the great Gordon Bennett race went through Carlow in 1903, a huge international event. Local laws had to be adjusted since it was held on the public road, and the 'Light Locomotives (Ireland) Bill' was passed on 27 March 1903 in anticipation. The race, travelling through Kilcullen, The Curragh, Kildare, Monasterevin, Stradbally and Athy, followed by a 40 mile (64 km) loop through Castledermot and Carlow, was won by Camille Jenatzy representing Germany. It drew an enormous crowd and many motoring enthusiasts needed the services of Benjamin Coleman.

Coleman's Paint and bicycle shop with a motorised Quadricycle parked outside.

As motor cars became more common in Ireland, Colemans installed petrol pumps on the footpath outside their shop in Dublin Street which became increasingly in demand since, at that time, it was on the main route from Kilkenny to Dublin. The family went into the bicycle trade in 1906, mostly selling 'High Nellies' which were the Rolls Royce of bicycles at the time. Benjamin and his son, Alfred, not only sold bicycles, but also repaired them which was skilled and labour intensive work.

As was the tradition at the time, Colemans was passed down through the male family line, with the sons helping out in the shop from an early age. Alfred's son, another Benjamin, took over at the tender age of nineteen when his father died. Coincidentally, he also died when his son, Walter was nineteen. Walter remembers the shop being a meeting place for lots of locals, who would call in to have a chat with his father in the evenings. The shop at that time was open from 8.30 each morning until 11.30 in the evening, six days a week, with only a few hours off in the afternoon on a Sunday. People

25

depended on Coleman's being open for petrol and there was no such thing as self-service pumps!

Some of the people who gathered in the shop at night were 'Sheriff' Dooley, Tony O'Boyle (Graiguecullen), Michael Dooley and Ger Mooney (St. Killian's Crescent), Dinny Flynn (Burrin Street), and Sean Lennon from Dublin Street. There were four or five people in the shop all the time and at 11.30pm Walter remembers his mother good-humouredly having to ask people if they had 'no homes to go to!' The radio was always playing in the background with programmes such as 'Sing Something Simple' on BBC and 'The Archers.' When RTE was launched in 1963, Walter remembers Paddy Kinsella setting up a tv in his window and a big crowd gathering round to watch it.

A long-term employee remembered with great fondness by Walter is George McCarney, who began working in Colemans in 1949 and retired in 1995. He was like a member of the family and was Best Man at Walter's wedding. Over the years, all the extended family helped out, including Walter's wife, Pat. When his mother died in 1988, it was the week before Christmas. There is no busier place than a bike shop at that time of year and orders had to be honoured. The shop could only close for two days before every member of the extended family came on board assembling bikes for Christmas presents. There were still thirty left to do on Christmas Eve!

Walter has many entertaining stories of things almost going wrong at Christmas. He remembers one event when the wrong bike was delivered to a family who had hidden it as a Christmas present for their child. The mistake came to light when another family came in looking for the bike they ordered for their child. Walter had to travel to a farm, retrieve a bike from the shed and replace it with the right one – all in time for the big day! He was regularly called out on Christmas morning because of some problem with a bike and he accepted that this was all part of the service.

Cycling took off in a big way in Ireland in the 1970s and '80s with the success of Seán Kelly and Stephen Roche. Racing bikes were in great demand. Walter remembers that on one occasion in the '80s he went to Raleigh in Dublin for a consignment of bikes in the morning and had to go back to get more in the afternoon. The petrol strikes of the '70s also contributed greatly to the uptake in bike sales. At that time, hundreds of people, mostly men, passed by on bikes every day going to the Sugar Factory and many will remember the bicycle shed at the factory, with the bikes hanging up waiting for their owner to return after the day's work.

An ad for Coleman's in the 1990s

The petrol pumps at Colemans in Dublin Street ceased to operate in 1999, coinciding with the introduction of the Euro. There was increased traffic in the town making access difficult, the through-traffic to Dublin was now taking a different route and several big petrol stations had opened on the periphery of the town. The bike trade continued until 2005 in Dublin Street, before moving to Charlotte Street, where many shiny two-wheelers were purchased and fixed, right up to the end of 2023. Walter's retirement marks the end of an era and a level of service which has almost completely disappeared in modern times. But his family legacy will live on for a very long time in memories and folklore of Carlow town.

A Passion for Watches

Interviewing Ken Tucker, one can't help but think that he is as much an institution in Carlow as the shop he has been running for the past seventy-two years! At ninety-three, Ken still loves going to work and is as excited about new stock and displays as he ever was. He is so obviously lucid and healthy that on a recent visit to the pharmacy to pick up his prescription, the customer behind him said, 'I'll have whatever that man is having!' and it's easy to see why.

Ken's father, Dick Tucker, was a well-known dentist in Carlow town and hoped that Ken would be a dentist too. However, having sat the exams for dentistry and beginning his studies, Ken wasn't happy, and his father came up with a new plan for him to serve his time as a watchmaker in Morton's of Nassau Street in Dublin. Before his apprenticeship was quite finished, Ken's father purchased Douglas' jewellers shop along with two other shareholders and set his son up as the manager. So, the young Ken had to learn on his feet – customer service, dressing the window, displays were all new, but Ken rose to the challenge and built the business year on year.

Douglas Jewellers was a long-established jewellery business, set up in 1850, but originally situated on the other side of Tullow Street. It moved to its present location in approximately 1880. Mr. George Douglas, the last of the Douglas family to run the shop, died in 1951. A question Ken is often asked is why did he keep the name? The answer is simple – it was a well-known and trusted brand and there was no reason to change it. People still come into the shop all these years later and call him Mr. Douglas!

The original Douglas shopfront with Mrs. Molly Douglas standing in the doorway with an unnamed employee.

During our conversation, Ken showed me a small, but very thick, notebook in which he has written the weekly takings of the shop since 1961. Every page is written in the same tiny, perfect handwriting which Ken still uses to write the tags for every single watch in the shop. His hands are as steady as they ever were and his attention to detail is absolutely meticulous. He showed me a display he completed this week with every watch clearly labelled and presented in the well-stocked window.

In 1989, Ken was joined in the shop by his son, Ivan, who had a flair for the business from an early age. The story goes that when he was thirteen years old and on holidays from school, Ivan was thrilled to begin working behind the counter. One day his father observed him serving a loyal customer. He didn't interfere but checked with Ivan afterwards what the man bought.

Ivan replied, 'He didn't buy anything, but he'll be back.' Sure enough the man returned and Ken went over to serve him, but he requested to deal with the young Ivan, and bought a watch for his own son from him. From that moment on, Ken knew Ivan had what the business needed.

Ivan and Ken Tucker receiving the "Irish Retail Jewellers of the Year Award" 1997 from President (RJI) Billy Whelan

Ivan served his time in the renowned Fields' Jewellers in Grafton Street in Dublin, before returning to the family business. Father and son have been working side by side ever since, assisted by Ken's daughter, Wendy, who also has a love for the jewellery business and his wife, Kay. Loyal staff have also helped to build the shop's excellent reputation over the years. In 1997 Douglas Jewellers won a prestigious national award when they were named 'Irish Retail Jeweller of the Year' at a ceremony in Dromoland Castle, County

Clare, hosted by the RJI (Retail Jewellers of Ireland). More recently, Ken received a lifetime achievement award for his service to the industry over his long and industrious life.

Over the years, Douglas' has become well known for sports awards and trophies. Ken proudly showed me his new machine for engraving even the largest of trophies – one of the only such machines in Ireland. His enthusiasm for the business is obvious as he recounts how the sports business is thriving, with cups, trophies and glassware constantly being engraved on the premises. Watches are Ken's particular interest, and he can list off all the brands, with the most expensive being Raymond Weil, costing a four figure sum. Opening a set of large drawers, he showed me hundreds of uncollected watches, dating back years and all carefully labelled – left in to be fixed and never picked up!

There have been a few close shaves over the years, as in any business. One story Ivan told happened at Christmastime a number of years ago, when everyone wanted their gifts wrapped and the shop was really busy. One customer came back the following week to report that when their son opened the box on Christmas morning, there was no watch in it! They were very understanding and all had a laugh about it, with the watch being restored to the box by the Tuckers immediately.

A new generation of Tuckers occasionally helps out in the shop now and the future looks secure. Ivan's son, Cody, and daughter, Tamsin, are already showing an interest, although they'll have to wait. Their grandfather, Ken, has absolutely no plans to retire. When asked to what he attributes his longevity, he quickly answers, 'The outdoor life.' When he's not in the shop, Ken is to be found fishing or gardening. He's certainly an advertisement for both!

Cheese, Wine and Haute Cuisine

It was a pleasure to speak with Betty Ryan-O'Gorman of 59 Dublin Street, where she and her late husband, Peter, ran *The Wine Tavern* and *The Beams* restaurant. This building has a rich history, with deeds going back to 1766. Originally 'The Blackamoor Head Inn,' it was later owned by the Duggan family, who ran a high-class grocery shop, before being leased by Drummonds (seed merchants) and finally bought by the O'Gormans in 1983.

Duggan's fine grocery story, 59 Dublin Street,
with Duggan's stationery shop in number 58 (photo IGP Carlow)

Duggans owned both 58 and 59 Dublin Street, with a stationery and toy shop in number 58 (later taken over by Ms. Bernie Hayes) and a grocery and bar in number 59. Many customers came in from the countryside by horse and cart, parking at the back of the premises where there were stables, accessed from Church Lane, opposite St. Mary's Church of Ireland. The ladies would do the shopping while the men retired to the bar! Duggans also owned a dispensary to the rear. An advertisement for the shop in *The Nationalist* of 1935 describes it as a 'Family Grocer and Wine Importer' selling teas, fancy biscuits, wine, Limerick ham, whiskies and liquors.

It was a tragic event that led the O'Gormans to Dublin Street. While they were living in Sycamore Road, Rathnapish, their fourth son, Marc, was knocked down and died from his injuries. Betty and Peter were devastated by this, and Betty told me she found it hard to continue living in the same place afterwards. Peter spotted that the former *Duggans* was for sale, with ample living accommodation, and the family, including new baby Marc-Ivan, moved there. At that time Peter worked as a sales manager for Odlums, but with the former grocery shop lying idle, a plan was formulating in his mind.

The following Christmas, Peter, who had always been interested in wine, decided to open *The Wine Tavern*, selling a selection of fine wines. The ambiance of the old building lent itself perfectly to its new iteration and the shop was very successful. After Christmas, when Peter had to go back to work, Betty asked him, 'Who's going to run the shop?' to which he replied, 'You are!' Betty rose to the challenge and found it a good distraction from her grief. Over the next few years, the O'Gorman family expanded to include two more children and the shop was so successful that a manager was employed – treasured long-term employee Esther Murphy from Leighlinbridge.

Gradually the range in the shop expanded to include a delicatessen counter selling artisan cheeses, Betty's homemade seafood salads, quiches and paté inspired by the recipes of Myrtle Allen who had opened her own restaurant in Ballymaloe. Betty was delighted when Mary Norton, who wrote a weekly column in *The Nationalist*, brought Muriel Gahan – a founder of the Irish

Countrywoman's Association – to the shop to compliment her on her homemade paté, which she had tasted. She wanted Betty to produce it commercially, but since this would have meant using preservatives, Betty refused as she believed in providing only fresh produce.

When Peter became redundant from Odlums in the economic downturn of the 1980s, the couple were looking for a new venture. The shop was being ably managed by Esther, and Peter was still sourcing fine wines and taking part in the harvesting of grapes in France. But a new challenge was needed, and it was Betty who set her sights on opening a restaurant, later to be known as *The Beams*. Having heard a programme on radio about a lady who had done a CERT course and set up in business, Betty wrote away for information and, while her three eldest children were in college, she went to Dublin from Monday to Friday to study catering. She also attended a course in Ballymaloe, taught by Myrtle Allen herself.

In 1986, Betty and Peter opened *The Beams* restaurant, accessed through the archway between 58 and 59 Dublin Street. The former bar, with some modifications, including a beautiful glass, vaulted ceiling, became a high-class haute-cuisine restaurant with French chef, Romain, serving an extensive wine list. A popular venue for almost twenty years, many artistic and prestigious local events were held there. Sadly, Peter died unexpectedly in 2000, leaving a huge void in the lives of his family members and the local community.

An interesting love story began in *The Beams*! On its opening, Esther from the shop asked if she might work there at weekends. One evening during the National Ploughing Championships, a Danish man who was in Carlow representing his uncle's farm machinery business, caught Esther's eye and asked her out. Once Betty had vetted him the couple began dating. Having kept in touch for a year by phone, Jurgen returned the following year and proposed. The happy couple now live in Denmark, with four daughters, running the machinery business which Jurgen inherited.

The Wine Tavern and The Beams in 1997

Although the business closed in 2006, Betty has been very busy. Her creative flair is now channelled into writing and painting at which she is very accomplished, being involved in local writers' groups and The Barrow Valley artists since its inception.

'No Mile Too Far'

The imposing building at number 18 Dublin Street is a premises with a long and varied history in Carlow town. The present owners, Thomas M Byrne auctioneers, have occupied this building since the 1990s. Prior to that it briefly housed 'Mothercare,' replacing the long established drapery store, Sloan's.

An ad for a shop assistant posted by Sloan's in *The Nationalist* in the 1960s

Sloan's was a chain store, founded in 1928 by Alex Sloan, with four branches in Dublin and fourteen others dotted around the countryside. Selling furniture, glass and china, as well as clothes, it served generations of Carlow people and was a valued employer of shop staff, administration staff and sales reps. In 1964, a fire destroyed the building and it had to be completely rebuilt. Prior to Sloan's, this premises housed Dillon's Restaurant, who rented rooms upstairs to a Mr. Berry, whose ad claimed that 'Rheumatic and Foot Disorders (would be) Painlessly Treated and Corrected!'

Byrne's auctioneers was originally set up by Tom Byrne senior who hailed from Glynn in Co. Carlow. The family owned a pub and farm. Both of Tom senior's parents died while he was still quite young and he was reared by his aunt. Having spent some time in London, he moved back to Dublin and finally Carlow, setting up his first business over Broughan's hardware in Castle Street. Selling was Tom's talent, and he loved meeting people. He first sold gas cookers, then moved on to furniture auctions, before getting involved in the selling of property. As his son, Tom junior, told me, 'No mile was too far for him' and he would travel the length and breadth of Ireland for a sale, even covering 100,000 miles one year in his car.

Tom's popular furniture auctions were held behind Kealy's of John Street, where he honed his auctioneering skills. As the business grew, he moved to number 15 Dublin Street, to a premises which was once the office of a weekly newspaper known as *The Carlow Vindicator*, before becoming Kinsella's electrical shop. When the opportunity came up to buy number 18, Tom and his son, Tom junior, who had joined him in business, moved to the fine, three-storey premises where the business now operates.

From cottages to castles, no property was ever too big or too small for Byrne's to sell. At one stage Tom senior even travelled to America with a portfolio of Irish property for sale. Tom's powers of persuasion were so great that he generated huge interest, so much so that he continued to advertise on radio in Boston, New York and Dallas as well as in the *Irish Echo* newspaper for some time.

Tom senior's name was known all over Ireland. His son remembers travelling the wilds of County Limerick with him one night in the early '70s. There were no Sat-Navs or Google Maps at the time. Having travelled all evening, they ended up going up a boreen and, looking for somewhere to turn the car, they were surprised to see a man emerge from a shed with a lantern. 'Is that you, Tom Byrne?' he asked. The man went on to sell his twenty acres through Tom and retired a millionaire, having remained loyal to the Byrne family business through many transactions for years.

The two Tom Byrnes, senior and junior

Tom could not be tempted by franchises or partnerships with big auctioneering firms. His famous quote was 'I want no partner, only a dance partner!' And he was a champion ballroom dancer! He encouraged his family to be involved in the auctioneering business, which is still the case to this day. Although Tom senior died in 2008, his son, Tom, continues the business, ably assisted by his wife, Anna, and daughter, Maria, along with loyal staff;

Fidelma; Catriona and Adele. Tom's late sister, Colette Morrissey, the first female financial broker in Ireland, formerly shared offices with him. Her untimely death in 2022 left a huge void in the family but her motto, which was read at her funeral, reflected her infectious love of life, inherited from her father; 'The goal is to die with memories, not dreams.'

Tom senior encouraged all his children to be involved in equestrian sports from their earliest years, believing that the discipline of looking after horses was a good life skill. His three children, Colette, Tom and Margaret, were all involved in pony clubs, with Tom going on to become a national showjumping star, representing his country on many occasions. He was captain of the Carlow team which, at the time, was the only team from Ireland to win a European championship. A serious injury from which he was lucky to make a full recovery ended his horse-riding days, but his six children continued the family tradition and the love of showjumping and horseracing goes on.

Thomas M Byrne auctioneers claim to be the longest serving auctioneers in the Carlow area. With a vast amount of properties to sell and lease in their portfolio and with the next generation now involved, they certainly look set to continue for many years to come.

Fruit and So Much More

Dooley's much-loved fruit shop, although closed since 1994, lives fondly on in the memory of Carlovians as a hub of activity where fruit, sweets, magazines and conversation could all be had in abundance. Many will remember that the largest Easter Egg in Carlow could be found in Dooley's window, a huge milk chocolate creation, decorated with icing. Although this item was actually purchased for advertising purposes, it was always sold, according to Pádraig Dooley, at the last minute, to some young man who was eager to impress his loved one, despite the fact that it cost the equivalent of a week's wages!

A painting of Dooley's shop by local artist Éilis O'Neill

Padraig's mother, Mary Dooley, opened the fruit shop at 62 Tullow Street, Carlow in 1955, the year she and her husband, Paddy, married. She had previously worked in 'The Bon Bon' café at the other end of Tullow Street, beside Tully's. Paddy had been running a fruit wholesale business since 1947, sourcing fruit in the Dublin Markets and distributing it throughout the county. During the war years, fruits like bananas and oranges from other countries couldn't be sourced, so after 1945, people were delighted to be able to access them again. Paddy was assisted in his wholesale business by his brother, Michael.

Dooley's fruit shop was much more than its name suggested. While there was a vast selection of fruit displayed in such a creative manner that Mary won several prestigious prizes, including becoming an honorary member of the Jaffa Club by the Citrus Marketing Board of Israel, it was also a local meeting place, with a predictable rhythm to each day. In the mornings people called in for the English newspapers, (the Irish ones were sold by Mary Kelly up the street.) There was a stool outside the counter where customers would sit and have a chat before moving on. Then, at 11 o'clock, workers from Doyle's of the Shamrock, Dempsey's and Lawler's butchers would come over for a mineral and snack, also staying for a chat, which is how Jean Hynes, the shop assistant, met her husband!

Since the Sacred Heart Hospital was just around the corner in Barrack Street at the time, some of the afternoon customers were elderly ladies who came around to Dooleys with a list of 'messages' for the other patients. But the evening was when the shop really came alive, especially if there was a good film on in the Coliseum. On their way to the cinema, everybody popped into Dooleys for sweets which were displayed in sixty sloped glass jars and weighed in ounces. Padraig remembers that when the film *Love Story* was on, the queue went from the cinema, past their shop and down as far as Reddy's! Other popular items were loose biscuits, Carroll's No. 1 cigarettes and John Players blue.

Among the regulars who called in for a chat in the evenings were Dessie Moore from Tinryland and Ciss Carpenter. Paddy Dooley would join them for the last hour of the evening before he and Mary would walk home to St. Killian's Crescent at 10pm each night. A notable customer was a man known as 'The Cowboy Whelan,' a colourful character who wore a Stetson and spurs and drove a large, American-style car with bull horns on the front. His home in Bennekerry had ranch-style gates and he called in weekly to Dooleys for a box of Hamlet cigars and a western magazine.

Paddy and Mary Dooley

Christmas and Easter were extremely busy in Dooleys. Mary was famous for her fruit hampers, which were assembled upstairs, over the shop, on what was always known as 'Dev's table.' The table had belonged to Ryan's next door, Mick and Bea, who had taken part in the War of Independence and the Civil War. Proud republicans, they hosted Eamon de Valera on many occasions, and he had tea at Ryans' table which was given to Dooleys on their death. They also gave a flag made by Cumann na mBan members who were incarcerated in Kilmainham Jail. The flag has since been returned to Kilmainham where it flies proudly.

As well as fruit and sweets, there was a magazine and newspaper section in Dooleys. At that time, everyone on Tullow Street went in and out of each other's shops and there was a silent agreement not to take another person's business. Therefore, Dooleys only began selling English papers when Bridie Mayer, who had another newsagents, died. They also sold Mills and Boon novels, comics and westerns, and ran what was known as an Argus Library where new, hard-backed books could be borrowed for a penny a week.

It was all-hands-on-deck for Mary Dooley's four children at Christmas and Easter. Margaret, Pádraig, Gerard and Thérèse remember having paper cuts from making bows for the hampers. They were also adept at using the 'pinking shears' which was used to cut zig-zag shapes with crêpe paper to decorate the edge of the windows. On Christmas Eve people would dash in at the last minute to get a box of chocolates for someone they had forgotten and just before closing time, one of the Dooley children was sent down to the Café Roma for chips to sustain the family after a long day's work. Then the turkey had to be collected (once forgotten by Padraig!) and the rush was over.

The three convents in the town, Presentation, Mercy and Poor Clare's, all had accounts in Dooleys. For feast days and special occasions, a large order for fruit, and occasionally chocolate, for one of the convents would come in.

People also left in money for the Poor Clare's and Mary would make sure that the nuns got goods to the value of it. She, herself, had a great belief in the prayers of the Poor Clare's and wrote to them whenever there was trouble of any kind.

Mary Dooley retired, aged sixty; her husband, Paddy having died in 1980. But rather than relaxing at home, she took to the adventure of foreign travel, first visiting her daughter, Thérèse, in Zimbabwe. She lived to the age of 83 and enjoyed lots of foreign holidays in the intervening years. Her contribution to the fabric of Carlow life will not be forgotten for many years to come.

Till Death Us Do Part

R. Healy and Son, undertakers, whose current business address is Pollerton Castle, has roots which go back to 1944 in College Street, Carlow. The business began with Dick Healy (Richard) who, although a baker by trade, saw an advertisement for a hearse for £100 and decided to buy it! Along with Paddy Kelly from Riverside, they started the 'Healy and Kelly' undertaking business, storing their hearse in Hynes' garage in College Street, opposite Dick's family home. Dick later bought Paddy out, and the business became R. Healy and Son – the son being Dick's only son, Pat.

Dick served his time as a baker in Slater's Bakery on Tullow Street, which was later bought by Crotty's. He worked there for thirty years, eventually rising to the position of Bakery Manager. Then, along with James Wynne, Thomas Stafford and Dick Carey, he opened a bakery in Montgomery Street, known as The Carlow Bakery, which specialised in wedding cakes and a large variety of breads which were delivered in vans throughout the county. The baker's day at that time began at 2am and the vans would begin their deliveries at 7. Unfortunately, the entire bakery was destroyed by fire in July 1976.

However, this setback didn't mean the end of the business. In the same year, the dormant liquor licence at 40 Tullow Street, formerly Kirwan's, was renewed by Dick and, having purchased the premises, he reopened the pub at the back, with the bakery operating at the front. The pub traded very successfully under the name 'Carlow Bakery Co. Ltd' until 1986. Dick's son, Pat, had left the bakery in 1962 to go into the insurance business. His motivation was to make money to marry the lady he had met in The Ritz Ballroom the previous year, Cora Lalor, who would become his wife and lifelong business partner.

Over the years, Dick and Pat ran the undertaking business side by side in tandem with their other businesses. At that time, funeral services consisted mainly of providing a habit, coffin and a hearse. When people died, they were usually laid out by family or neighbours and wakes would be held in their home. Coffins at that time were sourced from Prendergasts of Evergreen Lodge in Cox's Lane, who stored large sheets of elm outside their premises and made coffins on demand. Over the years the funeral business gradually evolved to include managing everything from the moment of death to the burial, including newspaper notices, Rip.ie, priests, singers, flowers and sourcing the grave itself. Nowadays, many people are cremated and that, too, is organised by the undertaker.

Gradually Pat Healy took over the funeral business, buying a premises in Graiguecullen as a warehouse for coffins as well as to house the hearse. In 1973, he bought Pollerton Castle, an imposing building on the edge of the town and, after renovations, moved his growing family in. By this time, the Healys had five children with the last one, Rory, being born after the move. The Castle was built in 1839 as a townhouse for the Browne-Claytons of Browneshill House. It included a large ballroom where they hosted many parties. In more recent years, it had belonged to the Church of Ireland and was divided into apartments. In these beautiful surroundings Pat and Cora reared their six children, as well as running the funeral and insurance businesses on site. As if that wasn't enough, Cora travelled to London to do a course in flower arranging, and from then on looked after the floral wreaths for funerals herself!

Dick Healy with his son, Pat, and grandson, Conor, outside Pollerton Castle

In 1979, Healy's built the first purpose-built funeral home in the South-East, which has since been extended to include two large rooms of repose. Their eldest son, Conor, who sadly died prematurely in 2005, aged 40, trained as an embalmer as well as opening his own insurance business. He was a proud member of the British Institute of Embalmers. Sadness visited the family again in 2013, when second son, Niall, also died, aged 47. Having spent years in England, he had returned to Carlow and was involved with the insurance and funeral businesses, as well as working as a barman. These were crushing blows to Pat, Cora and the family and made it very difficult to continue in a business that was so public. Pat retired from insurance but continued his involvement in the funeral business alongside his sons, Eoin and Rory, until his death in 2019.

Discretion is crucial in the funeral business and Rory Healy would not be drawn on things that go wrong from time to time, except to confirm that, on occasion, a hearse has broken down. At times like this, a cool head is needed, and Healys have coped with such mishaps with professionalism, always ensuring that the funeral continues in a dignified manner. The occasional person has also fallen into a grave, but thankfully without serious injury. When the floods of 1993 blocked transport between Graiguecullen and Carlow, it was necessary for one grieving family to have their loved one transported through the deep waters by trolley as the hearse could not get through.

But the most amazing story happened during the big snow of 1947 when it took a funeral three days to get from Stradbally to Graiguecullen. The road was completely impassable, and nothing could be done until the snow thawed and the traffic could move again. Thankfully, most funerals go smoothly and Healys can be depended upon to handle every request with the utmost compassion and professionalism. The business has stood the test of time and looks set to serve the Carlow community for years to come.

Rory Healy

Gone But Not Forgotten

A Dublin Street premises that has been the subject of much local controversy in recent years is the local treasure known as Murray's sweet shop of 25 Dublin Street. Sadly, this building was demolished in recent years, but lives on in the memory of Carlovians, as do its proprietors, Aidan and Madge Murray. Speaking to their youngest son, Oliver, a professional photographer who now lives in Athy, I learned a lot about the family history and this memorable shop.

In 1911, Patrick Murray, who hailed from Crossmaglen, moved to Carlow and for a short while worked in the Royal Hotel. He and his wife briefly rented 23 Dublin Street before moving to number 25, where they opened a high-class confectionary, with the staff wearing uniforms, and stocking luxury chocolates which were served with silver tongs. At that time, there was another premises accessed through the gates of number 25 where an elderly gentleman lived. Also, Carbery's builders had their yard at the back of the premises, including a lime kiln. Eventually the full premises was bought out by Murrays.

The original premises dated from the Jacobean time, and according to Aidan, who was an expert in history, the old Medieval Carlow wall divided his premises from the property next door, which belonged to Charlie Lewis, bootmaker. Some of this wall still exists. One of the many lanes of Carlow passed through Murray's and joined up with the lane behind the Irishman's pub and evidence of old cottages could still be seen on the right-hand side through the side gate of Murray's.

Patrick Murray and his wife, Kathleen, with their children. Aidan standing at the back.

Aidan Murray was the eldest of five children. Trained as a primary school teacher in St. Patrick's College, Drumcondra, his first teaching position was in Bray. However, the premature death of his father meant that he had to return to Carlow to look after the family and the business. Taking up a position in the Christian Brothers School (now Bishop Foley's) where he taught for over forty years, he put his musical skills to great use in the classroom, breaking up the day by teaching the boys to sing in harmony. He rewarded those who won his spelling and mental arithmetic tests by allowing them to choose whatever sixpenny chocolate bar they wanted from his own shop, before sending a boy down to collect it.

Murray's shop had an air of old-world charm about it. The terrazzo floor had been specially commissioned by Aidan's father. The counters and shelving were mahogany and there were huge mirrors – an attempt to make the interior brighter. The mirrors behind the shelves of glass jars full of sweets were also useful for keeping an eye on customers when the server's back was turned. On one occasion a man was noticed putting chocolate in his pocket while cigarettes were being fetched. 'That will be 20 shillings,' he was told. 'But the cigarettes are only 10 shillings,' he argued. 'Yes, but the rest is for the chocolate in your pocket!' was the reply.

To the left of the main shop was the ice cream parlour. Patrick had the foresight to buy an Italian American ice cream machine which was operated by a large generator outside. Huge vats of vanilla ice cream were made with milk from the Leix Dairy. There were farthing, ha'penny, penny and tuppeny wafers and, in the early days, people would sit inside to eat them. In Aidan's time the ice cream was as popular as ever, although it was take-away only. For many years, Aidan's sister Maureen ran the shop along with other staff. Maureen married Willie Bramley, watchmaker, father of Pat Bramley of Bramley's jewellery shop.

To the back of the shop many will remember there were two oval windows with net curtains and a door leading to the house. Aidan would sit at the far end of a long table where he could watch customers coming and going. He liked nothing more than to chat about music and plays and writing, and if customers had to wait, so be it! His great friend, Liam D. Bergin, was a nightly visitor. Musical evenings were held in the upstairs room with the piano, and writers like Eoghan O Tuaraisc were regular guests. Aidan formed a group of singers known as The Carlow Septet who were invited to sing all over Ireland and even featured on national radio. He also conducted the Graiguecullen Men's Choir and was instrumental in setting up the Old Carlow Society and publishing the first *Carloviana* magazine.

Aidan's wife Madge was an equally interesting character. While not greatly involved in the shop, she was very artistic and created wonderful window displays. In the 1960s, despite having four children, she travelled five nights a week to UCD to study Philosophy, History and French. Then, proficient in the French language, she brought her sons camping to France for long summer holidays in her Volkswagen Beetle! Once, when there was a ferry strike, she had the car flown over to France – her humble Beetle surrounded by Rolls Royces and Porsches! Aidan, having cycled throughout Ireland and Britain in his youth, stayed at home while Madge became an intrepid Francophile, reading up on different regions before embarking with her sons. When the boys grew up, she fearlessly travelled alone.

Murray's shop held several lifetimes of memories. A meeting place, an emporium, a place there was time to chat, where history was valued and loyal custom was rewarded. The gaping hole where it used to stand is a sad reminder of all that our town has lost and how important it is to record and remember the way things were.

Murrays shop on Dublin Street prior to demolition

Doing Business at Market Cross

The focus of this article is on a business that was situated at Market Cross in Carlow town. A lot of younger people will not be aware where Market Cross is, as it's not often referred to as such anymore, but in days of old it was the absolute centre of the commercial life of the town. In bygone days, the crossroads at the end of Tullow Street, where it meets Dublin Street, Burrin Street and Castle Street used to hold a large market every day. Dealers would set up their stalls with fish, meat, clothes and all kinds of goods on offer there. Carlow Castle Gate stood at this crossroads. In later years, it was often referred to as Duggan's Cross, referring to the business that stood proudly on the corner, currently bearing the name 'Bramley.'

Duggans of Market Cross

Pat Duggan came to Carlow in 1912 and worked in Doyle's of the Shamrock, eventually becoming a manager there. In 1930, he was ready to start his own business and purchased number 64 Dublin Street from a Mrs. Byrne for £850. Her husband, Michael Byrne, had been a bacon curer and lard refiner. Prior to that the premises was owned by Thomas Richards, ironmonger. The building can be dated back to 1712 when it was described as a brewhouse and gatehouse owned by a John Cooper, with ground rent being paid to Henry, Earl of Thomond.

To mark the opening of his new shop, Pat put a rather grandiose announcement in *The Nationalist and Leinster Times* stating 'Patrick Duggan begs to announce to his friends and the general public, that he has taken over the premises occupied by Mrs. A. Byrne, Market Cross, Carlow, where he intends to carry on an UP-TO-DATE GROCERY AND PROVISION BUSINESS!' He had recently married his wife, Kathleen, who was nineteen years his junior and a complete stranger to Carlow, hailing from Ballina, County Mayo. Within a year, their first child, Peter was born. The Duggans went on to have fifteen children, (fourteen of whom lived to adulthood) the youngest of whom, Colman, contributed to this article. With so many mouths to feed, it was surprising that Duggans made any money at all from their grocery business, as they were their own best customers, but somehow Pat and Kathleen made it work and managed to feed, clothe and educate their family very well. Two sons became priests in Seattle and one of the girls became a nun, with a wide variety of professions encompassing the rest of the family.

Duggans was essentially a grocery shop, specialising in bacon and ham. At the time there were a lot of small grocers within a stone's throw – another Duggan's (no relation), Restrick's, Leverett and Fry and Tom McDonnell's. With a house full of children, there was always work to be done and all the family helped out in the shop. Sugar and tea had to be filled into bags from large chests as well as dried fruits like sultanas and raisins. On Thursdays, all the shops in Carlow closed for either a full or half-day and this was when Pat Duggan cooked hams for the week over a stove in a very large pot. On Saturday evenings the shop was open until 9pm, which was very popular with farmers and their wives who came in to town to shop once a week, when their day's work was over.

Custom in the shop was mostly on credit and the Duggans ran a 'book' for people which would be settled on pay day or at the end of the month. Living in the centre of the town, Colman remembers that all the business people and their families went in and out of each other's houses in a neighbourly way. Young and old could call in at any time and all the children played together in gardens or on the street. A coal grate on the Castle Street side of their premises proved profitable for the young Colman as coins which had fallen from people's pockets and purses would drop through and could be collected from below.

Positioned as it was on the crossroads of the centre of activity in Carlow town gave Duggans a bird's eye view of everything that was going on. Colman remembers the excitement of Tullow Street lit up with Christmas lights on December evenings with shoppers coming and going, crowding the street. When Haddens introduced the very first gas-filled balloons in Carlow in the 1960s, they were a great novelty. Colman, like many children, let his balloon go almost immediately and had to watch the sorry sight of it drifting over the rooftops skyward. When groups of what were known as 'corner boys' congregated at the side of Duggans in the evenings, Kathleen would ask them to disperse, but if they failed to do so she was known to throw a bucket of water out the upstairs window which had the desired effect!

Duggans, like a lot of grocery shops at the time, also did deliveries, always having a messenger boy employed. Provisions were delivered to the Mercy and Presentation Convents and bread, free of charge, to the Poor Clares in Graiguecullen. A tradition at the time when a funeral passed by the shop was to close the shop door and blinds as a mark of respect. In Kathleen's obituary written by Oliver Snoddy, Duggans was reported to be a 'house where all were treated alike.' Kathleen was described as a woman of 'humble charm' who lived a life of 'resignation, kindness and optimism.'

Pat and Kathleen Duggan with 13 of their children

With the advent of supermarkets like 'Five Star' and 'Darrers' moving into the town centre, the demise of the small, family run grocery store began and in 1965, Pat and Kathleen decided to retire from the business and moved to 3 Court View. By then, many of their family were living away from home.

The premises was sold to Irish Life Assurance Company who knocked and rebuilt the premises. It was later purchased by the Bramley family who extended their jewellery business to encompass it.

A Bull in a China Shop

Popular local jeweller Pat Bramley's family has served the community of Carlow since 1946. Bill Bramley, Pat's father, was a watch and clock maker. He opened his jewellery business at 62/63 Dublin Street, having worked for Duthie's of Athy, where he served his time repairing clocks and watches. His father before him had been an engineer – an Englishman – who built the clay brick factory in Athy. The young Bill used to cycle from Athy to Carlow to dance in the Ritz Ballroom. There he met his wife to be, Maureen Murray, sister of Aidan from Murray's sweet shop. Having cycled over and back on Friday nights for a few years with his suit on the back of his bike, he decided to move to Carlow where he took up a position in Douglas' jewellers.

Bill and Maureen Bramley

Bill and Maureen married in 1944 and the following year they decided to rent numbers 62 and 63 Dublin Street, which had formerly been a greengrocer's owned by Mrs. Hayden and a boot-maker's shop owned by Luke Wynne. Without any money to invest in doing up the shop, they set about decorating the premises and converting it to a jeweller's shop. With a glass case donated by a neighbouring optician, and a large mirror behind a few glass shelves, they started by selling their wedding presents! It was all the stock they had to begin with. Since Bill had converted to Catholicism to marry Maureen in a quiet ceremony in Killeshin Church, he was out of favour with his own family and no capital was forthcoming to help him out in his new business.

By sheer hard work, Bill and Maureen made the shop prosper. Bill used his clockmaking skills and developed a thriving trade, visiting all the big houses in the region, dismantling their broken grandfather clocks, and bringing the working parts back to his workshop. Every part had to be made or fashioned to fit as there were no custom-made parts available. Then it would have to be returned to the house to be installed, with follow up visits if it lost or gained time. French clocks which stood on mantlepieces were very popular at the time and Bill was adept at fixing those too. Pat remembers his father telling him the story of a man coming into the shop who clearly didn't understand the workings of a grandfather clock. In his hand he carried a pendulum, insisting that it wasn't working! Bill had to patiently explain to him that it wasn't the pendulum that was broken, it was the clock itself, before arranging a call-out to fix it.

The large mirror intended to bring light into the shop almost ended in disaster one day. Cattle and all sorts of animals were brought to the market in Market Cross at the time and on one occasion a bull, on seeing his reflection in the mirror, entered the shop. Bill had to think quickly and somehow managed to get the bull to turn around and whooshed him out the door without damaging anything. There actually was a bull in a china shop!

Pat, being an only child, was always intended to carry on the business. Having attended Knockbeg, he was taken out by his parents after his Inter Cert. The plan was for him to go to Switzerland to train as a watchmaker. However, this plan fell through. Then, while he was on holiday in Holland, there was a red alert out for him. A policeman stopped the car in which he was travelling to say he was wanted at home immediately. Fearing the worst, Pat phoned home to find that he needed to get to Dublin post haste, as a place had come up in the newly built Irish Swiss Institute of Horology in Blanchardstown. The interviews were being held that very day. Pat made it to Fitzpatrick's hotel to be interviewed before the day was out and spent three happy years training in the Institute under two Swiss master craftsmen.

For the first nine years, the Bramley family lived in Granby Row, but then lived over the shop. Pat remembers playing with all the Duggan children from next door. Everyone lived over their shop at the time and Dublin Street was a hub of activity. When men going to the sugar factory would cycle by, Pat and his friends blew peas through a pea-shooter and tried to hit bald men on the head! The shop would shake with the vibrations of trucks coming up Kennedy Street. Once they were so strong that a Waterford Crystal bowl fell from a top shelf and smashed into a million pieces on the floor.

Returning to work in the family business, Pat set about improving the premises. Side by side with his father, he built the business and in 1971 he married Dympna, who hailed from Sligo. Sadly, his mother, Maureen, died in a car accident in 1977. The first major renovation took place in 1979, when the late Fintan Phelan contractors removed the whole façade of the shop and configured the two premises into one with a stylish marble front. Despite the almost complete demolition works going on, Pat's father refused to move out and continued to live over the shop. (Pat and Dympna had moved the business across the road for six months.) This almost cost him his life one night when, going up the temporary staircase, the handrail broke and he was fortunate enough to fall into a dumper full of sand unscathed!

The new premises was officially opened in 1980 by Des Governey and was very successful, with a wide range of clocks, watches, jewellery and glassware. In 1989, Pat and Dympna branched out and opened a stylish boutique over the jeweller's shop. Stocking many exclusive brands, the boutique was a must for the fashion-conscious ladies of Carlow. The shop was again extended in 1995 when number 64 was acquired – formerly Irish Life and Duggan's of Market Cross, and further renovations were necessary.

Philip, Dympna, Pat and Stuart Bramley outside their shop on Tullow Street.

Pat and Dympna had three sons, two of whom are now involved in the business. Philip, a Master Goldsmith, having studied in Manchester for three years and gaining experience with Taiwanese jewellers in New York, now runs the family business from Tullow Street (Finegan's Corner.) His brother, Stuart, manages the accounts and website. Their third son, Patrick William, runs ULAB Media Company. Dympna looks after all the business's social media accounts as she believes this is where the future lies. With their state-of-the-art shop on Tullow Street, the Bramley name continues the proud tradition begun by Bill so many years ago and looks set to do so for many years to come.

'A Better Buy at Haddens'

The name Hadden has been synonymous with the business life of Carlow for generations. Haddens of Tullow Street, Carlow, is a place everyone who ever lived in or passed through Carlow over the past hundred years or so will know and remember fondly. An outfitter for men, women and children, a coffee shop, gift shop, nursery equipment supplier – you name it, Haddens sold it, providing employment and training to generations of people who served the public there.

Frances Jane Hadden

Avril Hogan (nee Hadden) who has written extensively about her family, recalls that the Hadden family business began in Wexford in 1848 when

George Hadden and his wife, Frances Jane, opened a shop there. Sadly, after ten years in business, George died, leaving Frances Jane with four young children. Determined to keep the business going until her sons were old enough to help out, Frances Jane ran it single-handedly and duly handed it over to her sons, William and George junior in 1875. From then on, the business became known as W and G Hadden.

After many successful years in business, the Hadden brothers decided to expand to include a store in Dungarvan. Then, in 1909, they acquired numbers 15 and 16 Tullow Street, Carlow, which had been a drapery store known as Forde's. Ironically, it had previously belonged to a Mr. Henry Bankes, a brother of Frances Jane Hadden. At this stage, George's son, William, managed the Carlow business.

Many readers will associate Haddens with Victor Hadden, who was William's son. He, along with his brother, David, who joined him in business in the 1950s, ran the Carlow store until David emigrated in 1972. By now the premises extended from 14 to 18 Tullow Street and had been modernised several times. The fifth generation of Haddens, Colin, came home from London where he had been working in Harrods, to assist with the business. Victor, after some years of illness, had no option but to retire from the business in 1976. It was decided, therefore, to sell the shop to neighbouring Shaws, who own and run the premises to this day. Victor sadly passed away six months later.

In the 1950s and '60s Haddens was a major employer in the town, running a popular apprenticeship programme. Parents would pay a fee to have their son or daughter trained in Haddens. In return, the young person got their bed and board over the shop, a small amount of pocket money, medical expenses and membership of the YMCA where they could play badminton. There was a curfew, and exams had to be passed to progress to the next stage. A staff handbook instructed trainees and employees on what was expected of them. Apprentices 'agreed to be bound by the rules, i.e. to be of good behaviour, not indulge in alcohol, not let the company down with behaviour at dances and be a good-living upstanding person.'

The emphasis in the staff handbook was on providing good customer service at all times. Under the heading of 'When Greeting Our Customers,' came the instruction 'When serving our customers greet her by name if you can; if not, pass the time of day and, in either case, give her a smile. Our customer is our guest and yours, and we expect her to be welcomed; she will, as a rule, respond to a friendly approach which should not however be over familiar.' Although Victor, David and Colin modernised the shop, the dedication to providing good service never waned, and many people will remember bringing goods home 'on appro' from Haddens over the years.

Haddens was always a place where new ideas were tried out. People of all generations will remember that the first escalator in Carlow was installed there in the '70s. Prior to that, Carlow children were delighted with the introduction of the first gas balloons which magically floated at the top of a string, as long as you didn't let go! One of the first shops to introduce visits to Santa in the run up to Christmas, this tradition began in Haddens which was then replicated in many other shops. Victor Hadden had a way with words, and when the burglar alarm went off one Christmas season due to an electrical fault, Victor penned an article to *The Nationalist* stating that Santa had been doing his shopping there and that all the paper Santas had come to life, setting off the alarm. He also took the opportunity to remind customers that the new toy fair in the basement had 'the largest display of toys and games ever seen in Carlow.'

Victor used his writing skills to keep the staff abreast of how the business was doing, as well as creating a sense of community within the business where good and bad news was shared, with his staff newsletter *W and G's Notes*. New staff were introduced this way, and farewells were given to staff leaving or retiring. News of new developments in the business, apprentice exam results, as well as news about tax and the state of the economy were shared. A respected local historian, he had researched and written a book about local castles called *Come Capture Castles* prior to his untimely death, which was posthumously published by his family.

Countless staff worked in Haddens over the years in every department. Many will remember Miss Kelly who did all the alterations on her Singer sewing machine upstairs, Tommy Alcock, who managed the shoe department, Alec Stenson in menswear, Michael O'Toole, Mrs. McDonald, Harry Poole, Joe O'Brien, Betty Rothwell and so many more. Generations of families followed each other into employment there. From a time when there were coal stoves in the middle of the shop floor and tubes of money whizzing overhead to the modern Haddens Centre, the people of Carlow flocked to the shop which was one of the mainstays of the town centre.

Haddens, Carlow in 1967

It was a sad day for the Hadden family when their premises was bought by Shaws, a fellow Methodist family who had been their rivals in business for years, although personal friends. However, the name still lives on in Carlow and is proudly displayed in Tullow Street. The tragic fire which gutted the premises in 1984 left a gaping hole in the streetscape, but was rebuilt by the Shaw family, retaining the Hadden name. There are not many families who can boast five generations of business in any discipline, each playing their part in ensuring the motto, which graced Haddens receipts for generations, was upheld – 'It's a better buy at Haddens.'

Eye-Watering Ice Cream

The Jennings name is now associated with eye care in Carlow, but the business acumen dates back to Rita Jennings, who owned an ice cream parlour on Castle Street in the 1950s and whose son Bernard and grandson John continue the tradition of business in the centre of Carlow town today. Bernard's father, Gerald, hailed from Ballinasloe and moved to Carlow in 1939, just before World War 2 started, to take up a position as an accountant with Corcoran's. He stayed with Mrs. (Dr.) Donoghue in Leinster Crescent. At the time the population of Carlow town was approximately 7,000 people, as opposed to almost 30,000 now, so everybody knew everybody else.

Following an arranged meeting with a lady who was working as a pharmacist in The Curragh, whose name coincidentally was also Jennings, a love affair began which culminated in marriage in 1948. In 1950 Gerald and Rita Jennings purchased number 3 Castle Street and opened an ice cream parlour and confectionary shop. According to their son, Bernard, they had the first whipped ice cream in Carlow which was served in large sundae glasses – an exotic post-war treat. People still approach Bernard to this day and tell him how delicious that ice cream was. When people enquired where Gerald got the money to buy the shop, he proudly declared that he had won most of it playing cards, a very common local pastime of the day.

Mary Smyth, writing from America, has very fond memories of Mrs. Jennings' ice cream parlour and being brought there as a child. She told me that she still remembers the cushioned, wicker chairs and glass-topped tables where she and her mother would sit, having their ice cream treat. 'Whipped ice cream with red syrup poured over, made me feel so grown up and sophisticated,' she said. And also, 'Gerald Jennings, red headed with smiling face, cracking jokes at everyone on the street as he headed, on foot, down Castle Hill to Corcoran's. Sheer heaven!'

Rita Jennings on her graduation as a pharmacist

Four children were born to the Jennings – Oliver, Siobhán, John and Bernard – and the family lived over the shop. With a large family and a business to run, Rita needed help, so Gerald's sister, who owned a shop in Ballinasloe, sent a young lady to help out for a while. Della Ryan subsequently married Tom Clerkin of Stonehaven and remained in Carlow for the rest of her life. In 1960, the Jennings decided to move to the Leighlin Road in Graiguecullen and sell the shop. Rita was keen to get back to her profession as a pharmacist. At this stage, number 3 Castle Street was sold to Tony Pender who ran an electrical shop. It now houses the National Council for the Blind charity shop.

Rita worked as a locum in all the pharmacies in town, including Carlow Medical Hall which was owned by Sam McHugh at 2 Dublin Street, where, coincidentally, Bernard has run his optician's business since 1987. He remembers helping his mother count the takings and the float at the end of the day there after school as he waited for her to go home. Sadly, Rita died suddenly, aged 58 in 1979, while working in Athy.

Bernard with his son, John, optician.

Bernard qualified as an optometrist in 1980 and worked in Dublin for a year before returning to Carlow and setting up his practice at the back of Ruddock's shop on Tullow Street. Unfortunately, in 1984, Hadden's burned to the ground in one of the biggest fires Carlow has ever seen, and Bernard's optical equipment was completely destroyed with water and smoke damage. For six weeks he had no premises to work from, but then rented number 3, Dublin Street, which had been Brennan's Pork Butcher's. After practicing there for two years, number 2 came up for sale and Bernard bought it at auction for £65,000. This building, which was originally the Red Cow Inn, had been recently occupied by Tommy Alcock and was called 'The Shoe Box.'

The premises has 20 rooms and originally had a small garden. Guests of the inn would be able to bring their horses around the side of the building, through the gateway which leads to a cobbled yard, and let them graze overnight while they stayed there. Having restored the premises, Bernard moved his business from next door, where his son, John, has now taken over, using state of the art digital technology. Bernard has (kind of) retired, but still visits elderly people at home and in nursing homes to look after their optical needs.

An interesting feature of number 2 is that, before it was Carlow Medical Hall, it was known as McGrath's Medical Hall and was owned by the McGrath family, grandparents of Betty O'Gorman of 'The Wine Tavern' across the road. Clare McGrath was an accomplished artist and some beautiful oil on wood panels which she painted on the doors of number 2 are still preserved. There is an extensive basement which features a corbelled archway/tunnel which may have been a walkway back in the 1700's. Bernard has also preserved an amazing collection of bottles from the period which would have been used for medicines and lotions.

Section 2

'Carlow in the Rare Auld Times'

Introduction to 'Carlow in the Rare Auld Times'

For a couple of months, I interviewed older Carlow people who had fascinating stories to tell of their childhoods in our town. I particularly focused on the Dublin Road, stretching from the Court House to the top of Station Road, since that's where my own mother grew up and has always spoken of with such affection. It was a place where the front doors were left open all day, where neighbours loaned each other cups of sugar and children played happily on the street since there was scarcely any traffic.

The period remembered by most contributors covers the 1940s and '50s, and although it's only eighty years ago or so, paints a picture of a completely different Carlow to the one we know now. Families were large and children played together on the street. Men went to work while women largely stayed at home or conducted business from their home. Very few people owned their own houses, with most paying their rent to an agent who managed landlord's estates. People gathered around the radio in the evening and Sunday was a day for Mass or church, followed by football matches or walks. Shops closed for a full or half-day on Thursday and, should a funeral pass the door, they closed up and pulled the blinds.

I have really enjoyed gathering stories from all the contributors and piecing them together like a jigsaw which, when put together, brings a lifestyle into focus that is certainly worth remembering. An old African saying states that 'when an old person dies, a library burns to the ground.' The importance of capturing memories before it's too late can't be overemphasised. I hope these articles stir up memories in those who read them and that they take the time to pass them on.

The Greatest Actor in the World!

The Dublin Road in Carlow is now a busy thoroughfare, combining residential holdings with some businesses, St. Leo's Secondary School, the entrance to The George Bernard Shaw Theatre and culminating in one of the finest buildings in the County – The Courthouse. It boasts two hospitals – St. Dympna's and the Sacred Heart hospital and also two Primary Schools – St. Lazerian's and the side entrance to Bishop Foley School. In the mornings it is a hub of activity with traffic gridlock, but it wasn't always so. Talking to former residents, I learned of a different time, when Dublin Road was a vibrant, self-sufficient neighbourhood. Read on to find out about Carlow life in the 1930s, '40s and '50s.

On this street alone, there were three cobblers – a rare commodity nowadays, two dressmakers, three grocery shops, a Public Health Nurse and an Estate Agent. St. Leo's and the Mercy Convent played a huge part in the neighbourhood, as it still does, but back then, there were many girls boarding there and I heard stories of boarders who would send you across the road to buy a jam sandwich from Mrs. Price and of children being sent to the kitchen door to buy a bowl of dripping.

One very vivid memory almost everybody I spoke to mentioned, was the procession of black suited young men with top hats and walking sticks who made their way down the street every Wednesday afternoon. The clicking of the sticks on the roadway could be heard from the opposite side of the Courthouse as they made their way from the Athy Road. They were the seminarians from St. Patrick's College, sixty or seventy of them, walking with eyes averted, all in their late teens or early twenties. They spoke to nobody, and nobody spoke to them. There were so many seminarians in the college at that time that when the first students in the line reached the top of Station Road, the end of the line hadn't left College Street.

St. Leo's Convent on Dublin Road

Mary Smyth, nee McGovern, wrote in detail to me from her home in Chicago. A native of Leinster Crescent – the tall houses beside St. Leo's – Mary was an only child, the daughter of T.K. Smyth, a Customs and Excise Officer, and May McGovern, known as Miss McGovern, who was a teacher in St. Leo's. Mary's earliest memory of her childhood on the Old Dublin Road involves herself, her grandfather (Dada) and her friend, Michael Keenan, another contributor to this series. It goes as follows:

My very first memory of being on the Dublin Road itself includes Dada so I guess it's probably around 1952. Definitely before 1956, the year he died. Michael is in the memory. Firstly, we, the children, were not allowed to go out front alone: we had to play out back between our gardens. Dada had this old high-bike which he rode out to the Dunny Sleaty farm early each morning, where he loved to potter and grow things in their kitchen garden which is long since gone! Traffic in my Leinster Crescent era was minimal despite our road being the main road from Dublin to both Kilkenny and Waterford.

On this particular day when he got home he gathered Michael and me, telling us that there was a race-meeting in Gowran and that if we stayed quiet and sat on a couple of stools on the footpath with him, we'd see all the cars heading back to Dublin after the races. And you never know, there might be a surprise! We obeyed. The hours and the cars seemed to take forever to pass. Then Dada said, "Do ya see this car that's coming? The black one! The driver has his elbow out the window, and he has a big bushy beard? Well, that's Noel Purcell. Remember this. You've just seen the greatest actor in the world."

Another intriguing memory was given to me by Kathleen Carroll, now living in Donegal, who grew up in a house which was demolished in recent years directly opposite the side gate to the Court House – attached to the old Statham's Garage, then owned by Thompsons Steel Works. Kathleen's house, where she lived with her parents, brother Jerry and sister, Maureen, had originally belonged to the Richards Estate, and was one of the only houses on the street with a bath! She clearly remembers that when anyone on the road was going for an interview, to hospital or to England, they would come to her house, where her mother would be stoking up the range to make sure there was lots of hot water. After pleasantries were exchanged, the visitor would go upstairs, have their bath, and off they'd go.

Jerry and Maureen Carroll on a wet day on Dublin Road

Michael Keenan tells of a happy childhood on bikes and roller skates on a road which saw very few cars. To make some extra pocket money he used to climb up on the wall at the back of his house in Leinster Crescent where he could see into the Mercy convent grounds. Some boarders would throw a shilling to him and ask him to get them an ice cream from Mrs. Whelan's shop across the road, and to keep the change for himself. The entrepreneurial Michael got quite a few free ice creams in this way!

Mercy Convent boarders were a feature of life on the Dublin Road since 1916 as a way of educating girls who would not otherwise have been able to access second level education. Boarding was gradually phased out in the 1980s and the last boarders did their Leaving Cert in St. Leo's in 1985.

Lourdes Water and *The Student Prince*

Every single contributor to this series remembers a terrible day in 1951, which has gone down in local folklore as 'The Mullingar Crash.' On that Sunday, a party of eleven people travelled by minibus to see Carlow play Longford in the Leinster Football Championship. Having left Mullingar that evening, they only got a few miles in the direction of home when there was a head-on collision between their bus and a car carrying a Dublin-based showband. Five Carlow people were killed in the crash, with others taken to hospital with various injuries. Carlow was plunged into mourning.

Margo Lombard remembers the day of the funeral well. Five hearses made their way along the Athy Road to the Cathedral with mourners lining the streets. George Smith, who was co-owner of Whelan's shop on the Old Dublin Road, was one of the victims, along with Joseph Egerton of Charlotte Street, Hannah Hogan of St. Killian's Crescent, Thomas Hade of Granby Row and Edward Moore of Staplestown Road. A dark cloud hung over Carlow for a long time afterwards as the injured returned home, several of them relatives of the deceased.

Happier memories relate to the Operatic Society. Both Michael Keenan and Margo remember *The Student Prince* which was directed by Con O'Sullivan in 1966. John Brady was the Prince with Martin and Tom Brophy, John Kelly and Liam Woods also featuring. There was also an Operatic Society at the time in Castledermot and Doctor Seeldrayers, the church organist, used to accompany the musicals there. Apparently Fr. Waldron, a stern character, and PP in the Cathedral Parish, was endeavouring to set up a men's choir at the time and insisted that those who wanted to be in the choir had to join the Operatic Society. One story goes that he was passing a group of men who were waiting to be picked up by Carbery's Builders for a day's work. The men were standing near the presbytery when Fr. Waldron stopped to ask them where they were going. 'We're building an opera house in Castledermot!' was the tongue in cheek retort!

Newbridge; David White do.; Christopher O'Neill, McDonagh Qrs., Curragh; James Russell, Ballytore.

Carlow's choice

CARLOW Operatic Society have narrowed down their choice of opera for next year to "The Student Prince" or "Brigadoon." These two operettas were short listed at their meeting on Monday night last and the final decision will be made tonight (Thursday).

Practicaly all the cast for their Christmas pantomime "Cinderella' have now been selected and rehearsals begin tonight in the Bishop Foley Memorial School. A big influx of new members indicates that the Society will have one of their best seasons to date.

Marie

eting of nch will rs' Hall er 4 at

Monasterevan brigade were summoned to an outbreak of fire at Mr. Joseph Behan's farm at Ballykelly. Electrical equipment caught fire but only slight damage was caused.

Article in *Carlow Nationalist* from 1964

Margaret O'Rourke (nee Perkins) remembers being sent across the road as a child to get 'Lourdes water' from Miss McGovern who lived in Leinster Crescent. As previously mentioned, Miss McGovern later became Mrs. Smyth and her daughter Mary, writing from Chicago, picks up the story of the Lourdes water.

It's funny that you should have mentioned Margaret's memory of your grandmother Mrs Perkins (or maybe Margaret herself?) getting Lourdes water from Ma! I'd totally forgotten about that!! But suddenly I was back as a kid in 2 Leinster Crescent, on the second landing. There, carefully hanging around the banister knob, was this sturdy, large, dark green, thick-glass bottle, no label, the letters 'Gordon's Gin' protruding from within the bottle itself, an attached dark lid which was opened by unhinging its wire attachment, all of this surrounded by a basket-like tight-fitting container all of which could be slung over the shoulder by a beautiful leather strap for ease of carrying! It was always a forbidden-from-touch-by-small-hands 'heirloom' so for years I assumed it was booze. In my late teens I learned that my uncle Phil (McGovern) who had been in class with Aidan Murray had cycled from Dublin to Budapest in 1933 for the Eucharistic Congress. En route home they visited Lourdes (by bike still!) where they filled said bottle for my grandmother's bad heart. I never questioned where they got the empty bottle!!! I now clearly remember it being doled out to all when needed."

Unfortunately, the Lourdes water didn't stop Michael Keenan from breaking out in measles on the morning of his First Holy Communion. Dr. Larry Doyle was sent for, but there was nothing could be done, and Michael had to miss the big day, much to the disappointment of his mother. He received the sacrament on his own two weeks later. An interesting story was that there were assigned areas in the Cathedral at the time. The main body of the church was for everyone, but in order to sit in the side aisles you had to pay. The north transept, on the left as you face the altar, was for the very well off business people, while the south transept was for the middle-classes who were willing to pay six pence to the collector, Michael Lyons, at the door. Mass, at that time, was at 7.30am on a Sunday morning, so there was an early start for one and all.

The interior of Carlow Cathedral showing the north and south transepts.

Attending a funeral of a friend in the Protestant community was fraught. The rule was that a Catholic couldn't pass the archway to St. Mary's church without having to confess their sin. Margaret O'Rourke remembers her father, John Perkins, arriving home one day having attended the funeral of his friend, Johnny Craig, who produced many Gilbert and Sullivan Musicals in town. Mr. Craig was a member of the Church of Ireland community, although his daughter became a much-loved local Presentation sister (Sister Veronica). Margaret's father said to her mother, 'I'm for it now, Gertie, I'm going to have to go to Father Coughlan. I couldn't turn back at the gate with everyone else. I had to go to Johnny Craig's funeral.' On confessing to Fr. Coughlan, he was told, 'I can't help you, John. You'll have to go to the Bishop.' I assume the Bishop gave him absolution, but it's a lovely ending to this story that Mr. Craig's daughter, Sr. Veronica, was one of the first Catholics permitted to be buried in the Protestant section of St. Mary's Cemetery, alongside her father.

Major Fitzmaurice and 'The Irish Press Roadhogs!'

All the contributors to this series on the Dublin Road from the 1930s to the 1950s are agreed on one thing – it was the people themselves who made this street so special. Each of them was able to list neighbours from one end of the street to the other, signifying a time when everybody knew everyone else and children wanted nothing more than to play on the street or sit on a step with their friends from morning till nightfall.

A colourful character, whose offices were in Leinster Crescent at the time, was Major Arthur Fitzmaurice, a land agent to whom many locals paid their weekly rent. The Major was a large, stout man with a handlebar moustache, who wore tweeds and plus-fours with high, leather boots. Listed in the peerage of Ireland, he commanded respect with his loud, authoritative voice. He managed the estates of many local landowners, including the Bruens of Oak Park as well as George Bernard Shaw, who had several local properties. Outside his office stood his immaculate Wolseley car.

Leinster Crescent where Major Fitzmaurice's office was located.

Mary Smyth, writing from Chicago, shared the following memory:

It so happens that a family relative of mine was a tenant of GBS's in a house in John Street long before I was born – I'm guessing in or around the '20s. I never knew her. She was a Mrs Dunny, the young widow of my grandmother's brother, whose son, Willie, eventually owned and ran Dunny's Bakery and Confectionery in Castle Street in my babyhood. Willie was born after his (RIC officer) father's young death so Mrs Dunny had to cope with a large family and no breadwinner. Anyway, she paid her rent and made all her complaints to Major Fitzmaurice – of which there seems to have been many!! The reason I mention this is that quite a while ago whilst still living in Ireland (pre-1998, perhaps pre-1991) I listened quite humorously to a documentary on RTE radio called "Dear Fitzmaurice" which was on all of GBS's letters to the (old!) Major pertaining to GBS's property... Mrs. Dunny was mentioned.

A young Margaret Perkins remembers witnessing an encounter between the Major and Mrs. Duggan of Duggans shop in Dublin Street. The Major strode in and announced: 'I want a diary!' The proprietor, delighted to have such nobility in the shop said, 'Certainly, Major. It's so lovely to see you,' and presented him with a fine leather-bound book. 'That's no good,' the Major bellowed. 'That's a one-year diary. I want a fifteen year one!' and strode out again leaving Mrs. Duggan lost for words, since the man was at least seventy years old!

A much humbler character, who lived in Bluebell Lodge, was Mr. Paddy Bergin whose wife ran a tearoom called 'The Sugar Bowl.' Paddy worked in the Sugar Factory as a sugar cook and came to prominence by leading the workers in the infamous 'Sugar Factory Strike' of 1950. The workers had been promised that once they were trained to reach the same level of expertise as the Czech workers who had come over when the factory was being set up, they would receive the same wages. But when factory management reneged on this, Paddy, a member of the Labour Party, led the workers to strike, which potentially could have meant a lengthy prison sentence for him at that time.

Mr. Paddy Bergin

Paddy, a founder member of Carlow Little Theatre Society, later became a Senator, having served on the Urban and County Councils. He moved from Bluebell Lodge to Jerusalem on the Athy Road and finally to Dublin, where he reared his two famous actor sons – Patrick and Emmet Bergin. Patrick is probably best known for his part in *Sleeping with the Enemy* opposite Julia Roberts, while Emmet played solicitor, Dick Moran, in the long-running TV series *Glenroe*.

Mrs. Price owned one of the three shops on the Old Dublin Road at this time. A well-spoken, tall, blonde lady, her shop sold everything from a needle to an anchor. Her only child, Geraldine, ran a hairdressing salon on Dublin Street, called 'The Majestic.' Some of the most popular items in Price's were cakes from Dick Healy's bakery which arrived daily. Margo Lombard remembers being sent over by the boarders of Saint Leo's to buy Cleeve's toffee which was so hard you had to bang it off the table to break it. Apparently, back at the school, everyone would cough at the same time so the teacher wouldn't hear the toffee being broken in class.

Mrs. Smith's shop was another feature of the road, which was run by Cathy Smith after her husband, George, was killed in The Mullingar Crash. Michael Keenan remembers being given tuppence by his mother to run down the path after school to get the *Irish Press* in Smiths. At the time practically everyone on the road supported Fianna Fáil and the *Irish Press* was a must-read! In the afternoons, a big red van would career into the street with the *Evening Press*. Known to the locals as 'The Irish Press Road Hogs,' this delivery van was charged with delivering the evening paper in time to make sales all over the region. It was best to get out of its way!

Before the 'White Star' laundry opened in Montgomery Street, a 'laundry van' was another vehicle of note at the time. This van would collect linen from all the hotels and hostelries and take them to Dublin to be cleaned and starched. Horse-drawn floats coming from the station were chased by the children who tried to hitch a ride on the back, scuffing their shoes in the process. But, as a rule, the traffic was so scarce, that when the cold weather came, children poured water from the pump outside Ralph's shoemakers down to the Courthouse and let it freeze overnight. Then, somebody with studs on their shoes would skate first to make it really slippery, and hours of entertainment were had.

De Valera and Lemass Visit Carlow

Speaking with Old Dublin Road residents of the 1930s to 1950s, with their vivid memories of a Carlow long gone, is better than any history book. Three residents painted a very vivid picture of a torch-light procession coming down past St. Dympna's hospital and passing right by their doorways. Brush handles were held aloft with sods of turf lighting up the night sky. There were horses and droves of people cheering and walking behind, as a politician was escorted to address Carlovians assembled at Shamrock Square. In fact, there were probably several such processions as memories differ on who was being feted.

Having searched the archives, there were several politicians of note who visited Carlow in the 1940s – Eamonn de Valera on a few occasions, John A Costello and Seán Lemass. There were many more in subsequent years. Betty Ryan O'Gorman, who grew up in Montgomery Street and now lives in Dublin Street, was asked as an eleven- or twelve-year-old, if she would like to ride a horse in one of these processions, since she was accomplished at horse-riding. Betty, whose father was Secretary of the Fianna Fáil Cumann, neglected to ask which party was organising the event and when her father's friends relayed the story of seeing his daughter leading a Fine Gael parade in Ewing's pub that night, he was furious!

Margaret O'Rourke remembers her father, a quiet man, shouting 'Up Dev, up Dev' as a torchlit procession passed by. She was astonished at his uncharacteristic voracity, but clearly remembers Mr. de Valera proudly walking among a host of admirers. At Shamrock Square in 1943, he spoke from a platform presided over by a Mr. JJ Cuddy. *The Nationalist and Leinster Times* at the time reported *A Guard of Honour of members of the Garda Siochana was drawn up. Before the meeting commenced, a large gathering stood to attention while Carlow Pipers' Band played the National Anthem.*

Sean Lemass and Eamon de Valera in St. Patrick's College 1968 at the ordination of Bishop Lennon

In 1944, Mr. Lemass, who at that time was Minister for Industry and Commerce, also addressed a crowd at Shamrock Square and urged them not to forget the importance of casting their vote in the upcoming election. In 1950, a front-page *Nationalist* headline said 'No Welcome for Taoiseach!' reporting that Carlow Urban Council voted not to give Mr. John A Costello a civic welcome on his upcoming visit since he was visiting in a purely political function. There was dissension and disagreement, but the Taoiseach of the day was not given a formal reception.

Back on the Dublin Road, access to the daily news centred around one shop, Whelan's, later to become Catherine Smith's. Michael Purcell provided this lovely photo of the newsagents in 1965 with Mrs. Kathleen Smith standing outside, along with her daughters, Catherine and Carmel, and their cousin Annette Whelan. At the time, Whelan's was the main distributor in Carlow for the major Irish and British newspapers.

Annette Whelan, with her cousins Catherine and Carmel Smith and their mother, shop proprietor Mrs. Kathleen Smith (photo-Mick Purcell collection)

Mary Smyth, writing from Chicago, remembers the family who lived beside Whelan's. Mrs. Cummins, (known as 'Baby') was a sister of Senator Paddy Bergin who featured in the previous article. One afternoon as she was walking downtown, she saw a left-hand drive Cadillac convertible outside Cummins' house. 'I thought Elvis was in town, but it wasn't pink!' she says, as Elvis had just reached stardom. It wasn't long before news got around that Mrs. Cummins' sister, who was married in New York, had a beautiful daughter named Madeleine Cannon who was visiting with her boyfriend - a member of *The Royal Showband*. 'This', Mary says, 'made him even more exciting than Elvis! I was delirious with excitement without ever seeing either of them.' A fancy car was big news on the Old Dublin Road!

Music abounded as a means of entertainment in Carlow at this time. Residents have already mentioned musicals and operas which were produced to the highest standards. More locally to the Dublin Road, Sr. Joseph, Sr. Hildegarde and Sr. Celestine taught piano and violin to girls from the Mercy Convent in a building which no longer exists, but was roughly where the entrance to An Gairdin Beo is now situated. The sound of music being practiced by earnest musicians was a backdrop to the street. One of these students was Margo Lombard, who then graduated to organ lessons with Dr. Karl Seeldrayers, a highly accomplished Belgian Professor of Music who had come to Carlow as the Cathedral organist. Margo recalls a tragic event concerning his family. When Dr. and Mrs. Seeldrayers were away, their son, Paul, was playing on the roof of Drummonds factory in Pembroke and tragically fell to his death. The town was in mourning that such a tragedy had befallen their beloved musician. Dr. Seeldrayers, having taught generations of students in Knockbeg College and St. Patrick's, died in October 1996, aged 89 years.

The Magic of a Shop Window

Having received very positive feedback from many native Carlow people whose memories were triggered by these articles when they appeared in *The Nationalist*, I was pleased to receive the following memory from Mary O'Connor, nee Lyons, who grew up on the Dublin Road, opposite Whelan's newsagents. Mary remembers the excitement the small window of that shop held for the children of the neighbourhood. She wrote:

On a night late in November/ early December Mrs Smith would cover the shop window with newspapers – talk about excitement!! She was 'dressing' the window for Christmas! Next morning we ran across to see what treasures it held! We would tell Mrs Smith what we really wanted for Christmas and she dropped hints to our Uncle Martin (Lyons). Over the years I remember getting a tiny china tea-set, games such as Ludo and Snakes and Ladders, a Post Office set, lots of Annuals and best of all a cash register!! We played shop for hours on end and Mrs Smith provided lots of empty boxes for our 'shop'. I look at that tiny shop window when in Carlow and think what joy it gave me as a child at Christmas time!

A surprising detail, remembered by several residents, was that there were stables behind Leinster Crescent where polo ponies were bred. Mr. Paddy Hearns, whose family had a butcher's shop in Tullow Street and a farm on the Athy Road, bred prize-winning polo ponies there which were bought by the gentry throughout Ireland and beyond. This photo, provided by Joe Bohanna – a native of the street – shows Paddy with one of these ponies.

Paddy Hearns (right) who bred polo ponies behind Leinster Crescent on the Dublin Road

Mary Smyth, writing from Chicago, also remembers the stables. She describes a stable yard, stables and a two-storey stone building which held hay. This building was eventually bought by the Mercy sisters and became accommodation for boarders. She remembers a laneway and paddock behind the houses which ran right up to Guard McHugh's house, later to become Bishop Lennon's and now the home of Paddy Behan.

Dr. Larry Doyle was the local GP who served several generations of Carlow people. He lived in Dublin Street, not far from St. Brigid's hospital. Mary remembers that his wife, always referred to as Mrs. Leigh-Doyle, had a horse stabled behind Leinster Crescent. Mary writes:

A frightening toddler memory is one afternoon Anne Murphy (from no. 3), and I were watching Mrs Leigh-Doyle astride her horse in the lane, outside the stable-yard's big wooden gate. She was having problems with the horse.

It reared and threw her from the saddle onto the lane where she lay motionless. The horse took off. I don't remember any grown-ups being around, only us kids. I remember seeing blood on her head and me running to get Ma, and Anne running for her mother Mrs (Annie) Murphy. We had a cushion which was red (!) and Ma sent me for it, which she placed under Mrs Doyle's head. I believe at that time the only telephone in the area was in Mrs Donoghue's at no.4 Leinster Crescent. I think Michael Keenan may also have been with us and was sent to Mrs Donoghue to raise the alarm. We small ones were sent out of the way but I remember it took quite some time to get the patient from there, to capture and calm the horse, and to locate Dr Larry. Thankfully Mrs. Doyle survived.

Martin Doogue, who has lots of stories to share of the Dublin Road, was a first cousin of the legendary footballer, Ned Doogue, although his grandson Luke, who wrote a lovely email, explained they were actually related through his mother's side of the family. Luke wrote:

Grandad and Ned's fathers were first cousins married to two O'Neill Sisters, born in Argentina to Graiguecullen parents, who emigrated following eviction in late 1888! They returned in 1896 and gave birth to my great-grandmother on the ship on the way home. They lived on Chapel Street, Graiguecullen. The girls' father died in 1901, leaving a young family behind with his wife, who took on the role of breadwinner. The three girls ended up living on the Dublin Road in the early 1920s, Polly Horohan, Agnes Doogue and Annie Doogue (my great-grandmother)! And their mother followed suit, living in number 6.

Ned Doogue was one of the finest footballers ever to come from Carlow. He came to national prominence in the National Football League in 1954 when he scored a goal against Armagh. Micheál O' Hehir, who was clearly unfamiliar with the surname 'Doogue', announced,

95

'It's spelled D-O-O-G-U-E. It may be a strange name, but it will be remembered around here for a long time.'

1961 Carlow Team which beat Kerry 2-8 to 0-10 with Ned Doogue in the back row (fourth from left)

In his career, Ned won four senior football championship medals and two senior hurling championships, as well as giving great service to his club, O'Hanrahans, as a trainer. He retired in 1965 and died prematurely in 1972. Dublin Road residents are proud to remember him as one of their own and his memory lives on.

Mrs. McKechnie's Snuff Shop

In chatting with some older Carlovians, I have learned that the term 'Old Dublin Road' is not one that sits well with its residents, although this is what it is locally referred to. This, apparently, was a term invented by the Council when road restructuring meant that Green Lane became the main thoroughfare to Dublin. Prior to that, traffic travelled from the Court House towards Oak Park, under the arch and on to Ballaghmoon Cross en route to the capital.

This week I gathered some treasured memories from Joe Bohanna, whose home was situated opposite the entrance to Station Road. These houses were demolished in the 1950s. Joe recalled how he used to be sent by his mother to Mrs. McKechnie's snuff shop at the corner of Charlotte Street and Tullow Street. Snuff, a smokeless tobacco product which was inhaled, was a very popular item at the time, particularly with ladies. Mrs. McKechnie carried a wide range of snuffs of many different flavours and blends and young Joe was given strict instructions as to what blend his mother required. Common blends included honey, vanilla, cherry, orange, apricot, plum, cinnamon, rose and spearmint.

Another shop on Tullow Street recalled by Michael Purcell was that of Jamesy Griffin whose shop was situated where Lawler's 'Tiny Tots' baby shop was, beside Dempsey's hardware. By all accounts, Jamesy was a character whose 'laxative chocolate' was in great demand. It's hardly surprising considering he promised it would cure not only constipation but also indigestion, muscle and back pains, would help reduce obesity, loss of appetite, sleeplessness, dizziness, hysteria and a host of other complaints. It must have been great stuff indeed! Apparently Jamesy's shop-coat pockets acted as his cash register and hence the bulging pockets in this fabulous photo from the Mick Purcell collection.

Jamesy Griffin outside his shop, no. 90 Tullow Street. Photo: Mick Purcell Collection

Both Joe Bohanna and Michael Keenan recall the cinema being one of the main entertainments of the time. Each film, or 'picture' as they were known, ran for two nights and since there were two cinemas in the town, The Ritz and The Coliseum, you could go to a different film every night, if you had the money. At Christmas time, every boy brought a cap-gun along, which must have been pretty loud, not to mention the smell of sulphur! According to the men, the Ritz was the nicer cinema, but the 'Col' got better pictures, the downside being that the 'Col' had no double-seats at the back!

The Ritz cinema had three levels; the pit, the stalls and the balcony. Most young people could only afford the pit or the stalls, with the balcony being reserved for the elite who could afford to pay one shilling and nine pence. Joe recalls being determined to see what the balcony was like. Having collected bottles, which could be returned to shops for money, he managed to muster up the entrance money. At the kiosk on the way into the Ritz, his neighbour asked, 'Where did you get one and nine pence, Joe?' For one day only, he lorded it in the balcony, where the patrons had their own foyer and shop, considering himself the height of sophistication. Then it was back to the pit with everyone else.

Greenbank House on the Athy Road – the precursor to the Seven Oaks Hotel.

Betty Ryan O'Gorman remembers playing in Molloys field on the Athy Road. In later years 'Greenbank', Molloys house, would become the Seven Oaks Hotel. Mr. Molloy was an MP in the House of Commons for County Carlow from 1910 to 1918 and owned a drapery business in Tullow Street. He died in 1926. Betty remembers his widow playing the harp at musical evenings. There were two great hills in Greenbank's extensive gardens, where local children played. In 1944, when the Carlow team was crowned Leinster Champions, Betty and her cousins sat on Molloy's low wall and watched people walk, cycle and drive in their droves. Commemorated in the song 'The Carlow Fifteen' by Tommy Lynch and PJ Furey:

I'll never forget till the day that I die,
The crowds that went travelling that day to Athy;
They pedalled and walked it – excitement was keen –
And proud the supporters of the Carlow Fifteen.

It wasn't unusual to walk or cycle to a match in Athy or Bagenalstown or even farther afield in the 1940s and '50s. Some Dublin Road residents told me of a man called 'Jimmy Doogue' who walked to all the matches, even as far as Dublin! His shoes were tipped with 'quarter irons' which made a great clicking noise so everyone could hear him coming and were so well polished, you could see your reflection in them. The same Jimmy was also a champion billiard player, frequenting the CYMS in College Street and fending off all the opposition.

The Marble Hill Rovers

Such was the camaraderie in the Dublin Road area that the young men there even formed their own hurling team which featured prominently on the Carlow scene from 1934 to 1937. The Marble Hill Rovers comprised of young men from 'The Arches,' (where The O'Brien Centre now stands) to Leinster Crescent. An article on the club's inauguration described the team as follows:

Membership numbers fifty. A youthful lot, great promise, honours to come. The club wishes to thank the residents of the Dublin Rd. for their kind response to appeal for financial assistance.

The Marble Hill Rovers

In its few years of existence, the club did indeed bring honour to the area. Perhaps their finest hour came in 1935 when they beat their rivals 'Erin's

Own' in the Feis Cup Final in June. It was a particularly busy day for Paddy Payne of the Rovers, who was also a member of the Carlow Fife and Drum Band which played the teams out onto the pitch that day. He had to hastily drop his drumsticks, exchange his uniform for his club kit, grab a hurl and play the match at centre-forward. Other family names on the team included Donegan, Cooney, Hayden, Bohanna, Doogue, McGrath, Pender, McDarby, Walker and Hogan – all neighbours as well as teammates.

As well as hurling and football, Carlow had a wide variety of other sports on offer, although some were considered to be only for the elite. Rugby and cricket were two such sports which were played, at that time, where Heatherfield Court now stands, with the club stretching to the Oak Park Road. Joe Bohanna remembers leaning on the low wall bordering the road to watch the rugby matches to avoid the inevitable monetary collection that would be made from those on the pitchside. Paddy Mahony, who was Principal of the Technical School on Dublin Street, refereed the matches there. Joe also remembers throwing tennis balls back over the wall to the 'posh' people in the Tennis Club, one of whom he married!

Michael Keenan remembers seeing some of the Christian Brothers, who lived in the Monastery on the Dublin Road, walking to Dr. Cullen Park on a Sunday. He always assumed they were praying as they were shielding their eyes with their hands walking past the Rugby Club. He only later found out that they didn't want to see the 'foreign game,' the GAA 'ban' being in place from 1901 to 1971 prohibiting members from playing, or even watching, English sports, including rugby, hockey and cricket.

A vibrant Hockey Club, however, was thriving in Carlow at the time, playing their matches in the grounds of St. Dympna's Psychiatric Hospital on a pitch that was considered to be one of the best in the country. At least two international matches were held there over the years, one in 1939 and the other in 1962, both between Ireland and Scotland. In the '60s when club matches were held, one patient at the hospital is remembered for approaching every member of both teams and shaking hands with each of them, always asking the same question; 'How are you sagaciating?' (which is a fine way of asking 'How are you getting on?') Carlow members explained this routine to visiting teams who were surprised but accommodating.

At that time St. Dympna's Hospital was known as the 'Lunatic Asylum' and was hidden from view by enormous stone walls. The only glimpse most locals got of the patients was on the back of trailers on their way to the farm now known as the Braun site. Dressed in tweed suits and boots, men were brought there to tend vegetables which were used in cooking at the hospital. Otherwise, they didn't mix with anyone from the outside world which created an atmosphere of fear in the locality. That is, until the late 1950s when Dr. Bertram Blake took the helm.

St. Dympna's Hospital

Margaret O'Rourke remembers being at a meeting of the Carlow/ Kildare Mental Health Board where Doctor Blake announced that he wanted the farm sold. There was strong opposition on economic grounds as the food supply for the hospital would have to be sourced elsewhere. But Doctor Blake insisted that this type of work was not good for those suffering with mental illness as it was too isolated. He made many other changes which were hugely beneficial in bridging the gap between patients and the public, including taking down the high walls and changing the rules by which the dance hall in the hospital could be hired.

St. Dympna's had one of the best dance halls in the area which was regularly used by big bands. Dr. Blake made a rule that nobody could hire the hall unless they allowed a list of patients whom he deemed fit, to attend. This, along with developments in psychiatric medication, resulted in the dissipation of fear surrounding mental illness locally, and St. Dympna's becoming part of the local community rather than an island.

Betty Ryan O'Gorman remembers playing rounders in Shaw Park as a child. At that time it was just rough ground with a hill to one side leading to a high wall. This is where the Swimming Pool was eventually built. The wall enclosed another section of St. Dympna's called 'Kelvin Grove.' Betty remembers that a patient called Julia would regularly come to the wall and give the children apples from her wrap-over apron. They could sense her loneliness, although they were very young and always went to greet her.

Mario Lanza on the Barrow!

A very interesting former resident of the Dublin Road I spoke with was Martin Doogue, a ninety-year-old with a superb memory. With a photographic recall of every house on the street on which he grew up, he listed every single family. The Hayden sisters: Ollie, Carmel and Evelyn were champion violin players; Jack McDonald, the postman, whose son, Tony, was leader of the Carlow Fife and Drum Band; Mae Bunny, who worked in the Coliseum cinema and Paddy Coyne, who was an All-Ireland Senior Handball winner, to mention but a few.

Group of Mercy Convent nuns who taught in St. Joseph's: Sr. Euphrasia, Sr. Scholastica, Sr. Bernard, Mother Carmel and novice, Ann Holton.

Growing up right beside the Mercy Convent, Martin told me that he served Mass there at 7.30am each morning from age nine to fifteen and believed it gave him a great work ethic. When he left school, Martin worked in Kingstons on O'Connell Street in Dublin – a menswear shop famous for their shirts. He then moved to Arnotts and was promoted to buyer. Having learned his trade he moved with his wife and young family to Baltinglass, where he set up his own business, 'Kaideen Knitwear,' which is still a successful business today.

Another convent memory comes from Joe Bohanna who remembers having his First Holy Communion 'breakfast' there. It was a great thrill to be allowed inside the convent building and, while all the children ate buns and drank lemonade, their parents watched from a kind of balcony, before having photographs taken with the nuns in the convent garden.

Mary Smyth, from Leinster Crescent, remembers another neighbour, the singer Ernie Culleton, who lived in the house beside Whelan's shop. He had a beautiful tenor voice and sang at many local events. During the annual regatta, a barge would be anchored at the end of Cox's Lane and for two shillings people could take a trip up the Barrow to the strains of Ernie Culleton singing Mario Lanza songs. Mary says it was the first time she ever saw a hand-held microphone!

She also remembers Mrs. Perkins, who ran her employment agency from her house near St. Dympna's. Mary remembers getting help from her to land a job as a chambermaid in the Regent Palace Hotel in London as a student. Mrs. Perkins placed servants and maids to all the big houses in the region as well as to farms and industries throughout the country.

Dublin Road at this time, although only stretching from the Court House to the Station Road, had no less than a hundred dwellings, including a lane, now lost, called Bernard's Lane (where the entrance to Visual is now) which held eleven houses. Although living conditions for many were poor, there was no happier neighbourhood according to everyone I've spoken to, and everyone supported each other.

Mary O'Connor remembers the camaraderie on the road as she grew up and the kindness to children. Mary writes *I can remember doing 'messages' regularly for some of the women on the street. Running down to Nelsons for vegetables or to Joe Walker at Oliver's butchers shop in Dublin Street, or up to Major Fitzmaurice to pay someone's rent or to the lovely Kathleen (the priest's housekeeper) to get a Mass Card signed. Mrs. Smith even allowed us to read all the comics in the shop, as long as we didn't dirty them!* She remembers the Court House railings being very useful when roller skates became popular. She, and other children from the road, clung to them while gradually learning to steady themselves and take flight!

Milk was delivered by horse and cart from Oak Park by Mikey Lyons in big churns and poured into a container of your own. Margo Lombard remembers that the horse was so used to doing this job that it knew which houses to stop at without instruction. Food supplies came round in a van driven by Jamesy Hennessy, and with very few cars in private ownership, local hackneys owned by Doogues or Gahans were used when transport was needed.

When somebody died, Mrs. Pinkney was sent for. Arriving with everything needed to lay out the deceased in a respectful manner, she took over, and the family could rest assured that their loved one would be waked properly. Wakes were always held in the house of the deceased at the time and droves of people would visit to sympathise. Neighbours brought in food and crockery and the whole street was involved in helping the family through their bereavement.

Law and order wasn't a huge issue on the Dublin Road as everyone was very law-biding. But Guard McHugh, who lived in the first house on the Station Road, was always there when they needed him. At the time, Gardaí lived in the town long-term, and everybody knew them and their families. Joe Bohanna remembers Guard McHugh as a very kind man. When he and other young boys were playing in Paddy Hearn's field without permission, he said to them, 'I know you're doing no harm, boys. If Paddy comes, jump over my wall, run through the garden and hide in the station.'

Two Carlow Gardaí of note: Garda Broughall (left) and Garda McHugh

They say 'it takes a village to raise a child,' and in this case the village was the Dublin Road. I'm delighted that so many people have expressed their pleasure at reading these articles about a treasured place in the history of Carlow town. There's much we can learn from the neighbourliness of this humble street.

Section 3

'Russell's Registry'

Introduction – Russell's Registry

Many older Carlovians will remember a time when looking for a job involved a visit to a local employment agency. These agencies found positions as cooks, cleaners, stable-hands and other domestic staff for people in large houses and estates, with the proprietor becoming the trusted intermediary between employer and employee. One such agency was established in Carlow in 1900 by my great-grandmother, Margaret Russell and was continued right up to the 1970s by her daughter, my grandmother, Gertrude Perkins.

Piecing together the letters and correspondence that survive from my grandmother's time has been fascinating, especially nowadays when we rarely see a handwritten letter. All the letters of application and references were penned in beautiful script on headed paper. Some tell sad stories of being treated badly, others are letters of complaint. Many references contain words like 'clean' and 'respectable' which we would never use in modern times. But all of them tell a story of another time, stories that shouldn't be forgotten.

I hope that these articles will open a window to Carlow's past, to a way of life that no longer exists, but which reveals much about the social history of our town and country. While it is the story of my own ancestors, it's also much more than that. It's a story of strong women, of survival and reinvention and of service to employers and to the community. As Nelson Mandela said; 'It is the difference we have made in the lives of others that will determine the significance of the life we lead.' I think 'Russell's Registry' made a big difference in the lives of many people. I hope readers will enjoy its unfolding story and that it invokes memories of days gone by.

'Sunday-Go-To-Meeting-Hat'

The smartly dressed, elderly lady I remember as my Granny Perkins, was always an enigma to me. A resourceful lady of impeccable manners, she was both respected and feared by those who knew her. As a small child, I remember walking to town with her, in tweed skirt, mink necklet and 'Sunday go to Meeting Hat.' Elderly men would tip their caps deferentially, muttering 'Mrs. Perkins' as they passed, to which Granny would reply in confident tones: 'Good morning! Lovely day today.'

She cultivated a regal air, with her head held high, and was known to grandly use the phrase 'My good man!' She frowned on people who congregated in the street, referring to them as 'corner boys!' and coached the entire family on the need to look 'respectable' in public places. And yet, that same lady was a proud Carlovian, proud of her late husband's service in the Civil War. She was discreetly generous to those less fortunate, always keeping cast-offs and leftover food for regular callers to her door, and had a strong faith with diligent religious observance. Yet, in business she was incisive and was known to have an acerbic, quick wit when the need arose.

Curious to know the influences that formed this woman of paradox who died when I was seventeen, but who had been incrementally lost to us for a decade before that, I delved into her formative years and the curious mixture of privilege and hardship that formed her. It's the story of a lifetime spent largely within a mere square mile, but with a sphere of influence that reached well beyond. A complicated mixture of loyalties and attitudes, hers was a modest life lived on the edges of gentility, with an undercurrent of pain and loss stoically endured and rarely spoken of.

Margaret, Gertrude Russell's mother, was both carer and provider to a household to which Gertie was the fourth child, the first from a second marriage, born to Margaret and Joseph Gunn Russell on June 22nd 1900. Margaret was a woman of indomitable spirit, which was tested many times in her early life. Joseph, described in his obituary as a man of 'kindly disposition', was Margaret's second husband, a piano-tuner from a family of some standing – 'Gunn brothers,' piano makers based in Dublin – who were responsible for establishing the Gaiety Theatre in Dublin.

'Gertie,' as she was known within the family, was her father's only child, but had three step-sisters from her mother's first marriage to Hugh Ferguson, a professional pianist: Margaret was obviously drawn to musicians, possibly their artistic nature complemented her own practicality. He and Margaret (nee O'Dwyer) married in 1883 in Kingstown, Dublin (now Dun Laoghaire) in the Catholic Church, leading to disownment by his Presbyterian family, since he had converted in order to marry her. They had five children within two years – triplets and twins – all of whom died except Ada. It must have been with trepidation, therefore, that the young couple went on to have three more children, Maggie, Julia, and a girl called Ginny. Sadly, tragedy struck again when Ginny died aged four.

To add to Margaret's misfortune, Hugh Ferguson contracted Tuberculosis, for which there was no cure, and died within days of his youngest daughter in the late 1890's. Although her heart must have been broken, Margaret had a family to look after and there was no widow's pension or state assistance of any kind. It's unclear why she brought her three daughters to live in Carlow, where she originally set up a small confectionary shop on Tullow

Street. Unfortunately, this business failed and, since the family lived over the shop, the ever resourceful Margaret immediately set up another business, this time an employment agency for the placement of servants in big houses, colleges and farms. During this period she had no money to pay the rent, and the bailiffs came to evict her, arriving when she was ill with jaundice. The bailiff, a man named Brophy, instructed the men to take not only the furniture and effects, but the bed she was lying in. Pitying her, they refused to do this, but she was left with nothing.

Margaret wrote to her father for help – a Mr. O'Dwyer who was a wealthy coal-merchant in Dublin, father to fifteen children – but was amazed to get no reply. She subsequently discovered that he had died and she hadn't been notified. It seems that her family decided not to tell her since her husband and child had died so recently and they felt it would be too much for her. Somehow, probably with the help of other family members, she managed to rent another house in Brown Street and set up in business again, while also keeping boarders. She gradually acquired two hackney cars with two live-in drivers as well.

Margaret's three-storey house was around the corner from the Royal Hotel, where many business people and commercial travellers stayed. When they had an overflow, a porter would come around and ask her if she had any room. On one such night a gentleman who was a regular guest at the hotel had arrived when the hotel was full. Joseph Gunn Russell, a piano-tuner from Dublin in his late thirties, was sent around to her. Initially he stayed about a week, while he tended to pianos and organs locally, but he returned again and again and they were married in 1899 in Carlow Cathedral. The following year, their daughter Gertrude was born.

While very different in personality, Margaret and Joseph complemented each other well. They both enjoyed music and reading. At night they would sit each side of the fire, with Joseph reading the classics or *National Geographic*, while Margaret read her everyday law primer entitled *Law for the Millions*. She became so knowledgeable about law that people used to call to consult her on legal matters, prompting a local solicitor to comment:

'I believe you're taking some of my business, Mrs. Russell,'

to which she replied:

'Yes, but I believe my rates are better!

Gertie's childhood was spent in Brown Street, Carlow with her mother and father and three stepsisters, the youngest of whom, Julia, was ten years her senior. While she originally went to the Presentation Convent school nearby, she told the story that a wealthy aunt, her father's sister, called Mrs. Mary Pakenham, visited and was appalled that she was attending 'the poor school.' From that day on she was educated by the Mercy sisters in the fee-paying St. Leo's school, funded by Mr. and Mrs. Frank Pakenham of Clare Street, Dublin. Mr. Pakenham was a dentist at the Royal College of Surgeons, a member of the professional middle class.

Gertie had a close relationship with her father, sometimes accompanying him to tune pianos. She obviously paid attention, because she told a story that much later in her life a friend had employed someone to tune her piano, but they had given it up as a lost cause. Gertie rolled up her sleeves and did it for them, note perfect. Joseph was also very much a part of giving Gertie her extensive vocabulary. When she was old enough to read, she would sit, reading with her parents in the evening. When she came upon a word she didn't understand, she would ask her father what it meant. Eager to get back to her book, she was frustrated when he would say:

'Now, Gertie, put that word into three sentences for me and you'll never forget it.'

Gertrude Perkins in later years

Some of Margaret's earliest ads, which were under the name 'Ferguson's Registry' featured in national papers, such as the *Irish Independent* as well as regional newspapers as far flung as *The Western People* which circulated in Mayo, Sligo and Roscommon, and read as follows:

Ladies requiring good, reliable, country servants, not afraid of work, will get suited at once at Mrs. Ferguson's Registry, Tullow St. Carlow. Try here for good servants.

Freeman's Journal July 04, 1898

Employers try Ferguson's Registry, Carlow, for reliable farm labourers and servant boys for colleges, hotels, etc., England, Ireland, Scotland.

Western People Feb 10, 1912

However, Margaret's indefatigable spirit and confidence is, perhaps, best seen in her local ads, which she placed weekly in *The Nationalist and Leinster Times* newspaper, which was published in Carlow:

Russells' Registry, Carlow, continues first in Ireland for supplying employers with reliable domestics, and providing men and women servants with suitable situations. They lead, others follow.

Nationalist and Leinster Times May 04, 1918

Joseph and Margaret Russell

This line, 'They lead, others follow,' became the catchphrase for her business dealings and perhaps her life as she became a successful businesswoman in a man's world.

Death and Spanish Flu

While Margaret (Ferguson) was running her small shop on Tullow Street, something terrible happened. Here is an excerpt from the account which appeared in *The Nationalist and Leinster Times* on March 26th 1898:

SAD BURNING FATALITY IN CARLOW.

On Sunday evening a little girl named Anastatia Byrne, aged between nine and ten years, the daughter of a labouring man named Wm. Byrne, of Pollerton Road, Carlow, came by her death under circumstances of a peculiarly sad nature.... From Mrs Ferguson's statement it seems she and her daughter were taking their tea about 7 o'clock on Sunday evening in the kitchen off the shop, and the deceased was in the same apartment with them about four feet from the fire. Whilst at tea a customer entered the shop which occasioned Mrs. Ferguson's leaving the kitchen. At the same time the latter's little daughter left the kitchen also, and in a short time returned, and to her horror saw the deceased child in flames. She screamed to her mother who resumed to the kitchen at once from the shop and saw the deceased enveloped in flames near the fire. Mrs Ferguson did everything she possibly could to extinguish the fire and in doing so got her hands very severely burned.'

A short time after this sad happening, due to inability to pay her rent, Margaret was evicted. She relocated to Brown Street where she began to run her new business, known for a period as 'Ferguson's Registry'. However, on remarrying Mr. Joseph Russell in 1899, she began to advertise under the name of 'Russell's Registry.' Two of her ads in this transitionary period read:

Ferguson and Russell's Registry Carlow, continues first for immediate situations and good wages. They lead, others follow. (1901)

Ladies requiring reliable country servants, not afraid of work, suited immediately at Ferguson's Registry. They lead, others follow.

Employment law was very different then to now, and discriminatory ads on the basis of gender and religion were commonplace:

Wanted immediately, a number of Protestant and Catholic Servants; good wages. Ferguson's Registry, Carlow. (1899)

Duckett's Grove

Margaret's new husband, Joseph Gunn Russell, was a piano tuner of some repute and while Margaret ran her businesses from the house, he continued to tune and service pianos and organs both in Dublin and locally. One country house Joseph is known to have had on his books was 'Duckett's Grove,' a large 18th century mansion, complete with turrets and Gothic towers. Situated a few miles outside Carlow, and, prior to the Civil War, inhabited by the Duckett family, it had many servants and up to eight or even nine pianos. In a letter to the *Nationalist and Leinster Times* in 1974, Ernest O'Rourke-

Glynn from Athy wrote that he would travel to Duckett's Grove with his father who gave magic lantern lectures and animated picture shows there. He went on to say:

On these occasions two other Carlovians we used to meet at Duckett's Grove were a man named Purcell, coach painter and coach builder, who actually did some work for Bianconi, and a man called Gunn Russell, who seemed to be responsible for all the pianos – I seem to recall eight or nine pianos.

Joseph used to go out for a stroll around town in the evening, sometimes popping in to tune someone's piano, unbeknownst to Margaret. The fees for these unofficial assignations went into his own pocket, rather than the family coffers! On a couple of occasions, his daughter Gertie, who later took over the agency, happened upon him coming out of one of these houses, so much so that he began to jokingly call her 'The Ubiquitous Gertie.'

While Margaret was determined and industrious, it seems Joseph was hard-working and affable. Local people were known to say:

'Mrs. Russell is a great business woman, but Mr. Russell is a gentleman.'

A letter of good-tempered complaint which he penned to a Council official by the name of Kelly, which was printed in *The Nationalist* newspaper in 1911 gives an insight to his personality:

My Dear Mr. Kelly – I would be much obliged if you would kindly bring before the Council's meeting the unsatisfactory lighting of the town. It is almost impossible to find one's way through the streets. One night I was out driving and some boys took advantage of the extreme darkness and stoned me and broke one of my lamps. If any accident occurs to me again I will hold the Urban Council liable for same. It is simply absurd paying rates for lighting and not getting it (laughter). Yours very truly,

   Gunn Russell

Margaret and Joseph's house in Brown Street was a fine house by the standards of the day, with five bedrooms. Margaret supplemented the family income by keeping overflow guests from the Royal Hotel on Dublin Street. She also kept boarders – respectable men only!

RESPECTABLE young men can have comfortable board and lodgings on moderate terms, by applying to Russell's Registry, Carlow (1910)

Margaret also acquired two hackney cars and reared her four surviving daughters in relative comfort. It would seem, then, that my grandmother Gertrude, who eventually took over the agency, grew up in a happy, stable home, where she learned the value of education and hard work. She was indulged by her gentle, well-read father, while learning by example from her shrewd, resourceful mother. Her trail-blazing, superior attitude was surely learned at the feet of the woman who penned the words: 'They lead, others follow.'

There were great events of the time that made a lasting impression on the young Gertie. When she was twelve, one of the biggest maritime disasters in history occurred – the sinking of the Titanic. Although far removed from it in Carlow, she was quite affected by it and often spoke of the human toll which she had read about in the national papers. While the local paper had advertised tickets for both the 'Olympic' and the 'Titanic' in 1911 with the proud boast of 'unsurpassed accommodation for First, Second and Third Class passengers at low rates' (July 22, 1911), it was only a few short months when the heading 'Titanic Disaster Reflections' appeared with an account of how the tragedy unfolded. The following curt notice from the Post Office was also featured in *The Nationalist* of November 1912:

The Post Office will pay no compensation for registered letters lost in the Titanic, as the Court of Inquiry found that the wreck was due to cause beyond control. Compensation is confined to letters and parcels insured, the Post Master General told Mr. Ffrench in Parliament yesterday.

Margaret Russell and her daughter, Gertie

Gertie lived through World War One, or the 'Great War' as it was known in Ireland and England, as a teenager. Its effects were mostly felt in Carlow as supply issues, though it may have reduced rations for the boarders as well as interrupting the availability of young men and women for Margaret's business. Gertie's joy at the Great War ending was, perhaps, tempered by the arrival of the Spanish Flu, which she herself caught in 1918. She often recalled there being five or six coffins laid out in the Cathedral, which was a stone's throw from her house, on the same evening, many of them young people. When she herself contracted it, she was very ill. A story she often told was that, when she was recovering and had gotten very thin, she went out to get some air, but unable to walk, she half-sat on the windowsill. As she told it: 'A kind of ignorant woman' passed by as Gertie's mother was pleading with her to come back in.

'Ye needn't bother, Missus,' said the woman. 'Shure look at her – I'd say that one more clean shirt will do her!'

In fact, Gertie recovered and lived into her 82nd year, overcoming many trials and illnesses, following her mother and sister into the family business and rearing a family of her own.

Gertie – A Survivor Once Again

Having left school at eighteen years, Gertie travelled to London to stay with her stepsister, Julia, whose husband was a publican in London. On her return to Ireland she acquired a position as a governess with a well-to-do family called Kelly in Dun Laoghaire, County Dublin. At that time a lot of the daughters of well-off people were educated at home until they were old enough for boarding school. This was as much about ensuring girls turned into 'ladies' as it was about education.

Gertie was quite lonely in this position, with her movements being very restricted. She recounted that one of her duties was to take the girls for a walk on the pier each day, but while she would have liked to take them on the new pier which was a hive of activity, she was instructed to take them on the old pier where she would meet only a few elderly walkers.

Another story she told of this period, and a testament to her confidence and bravery, was of being out swimming alone one day in Dun Laoghaire. Having grown up in an inland county, she was unaccustomed to swimming in the sea, most likely having learned to swim in the local river, the Barrow. She was close to rocks and felt safe but suddenly realised she was being pulled downwards. With all her might she tried to swim ashore, but couldn't make any progress. She had become caught in a whirlpool. A male passer-by rescued her and told her that it was well known locally that the sea was treacherous at that spot. She was badly shaken by this incident and was reluctant to ever swim in the sea again.

Gertie's three step-sisters couldn't have been more different from each other. Maggie, who worked for a time as a governess to the Marquis McSweeney's family, spent most of her life helping with her mother's employment agency which was doing a thriving business. She also looked after the hackney car business with her husband, Mr. Jim Ferris. She was an elegant lady, noted for her style and fine clothes.

Gertie's family: Back- Maggie and Ada, Front – Julia, Joseph, Julia's children Jackie and Kate, mother, Margaret and Gertie, aged approximately twenty.

However, Maggie had another interesting occupation, for which she was renowned locally, as a psychic – she would read people's cards and, with a degree of accuracy, tell them what was in store for them. She read the tea leaves and purported to communicate with spirits. During both World Wars, people whose sons had been fighting and were missing in action, would come to see Maggie. Smart motor cars and coaches would be seen parked outside the house in Brown Street, while ladies in fine dresses would slip through the door to consult her. She would read the cards for them and pinpoint on the map where their sons were, and whether they were still alive. It was widely held that she was accurate in her pronouncements. But the most poignant story concerned a member of her own family.

Gertie's other stepsister, Julia, was living in London with a family of her own. She was a spirited, outgoing lady. Her husband Mr. Jack O'Connor's family owned and ran several public houses in the West End. In 1914 Julia made a trip home, bringing her baby, Teddy O'Connor. She stayed for a period of time in the family home in Brown Street, and the night before she returned to England she asked her sister Maggie to read the cards for her. It was all quite jovial and there was some laughter when Maggie said that there was no travel on the cards for Julia. Since she was due to go home the next day, Julia said,

'Nothing will stop me getting on that boat tomorrow.'

But she was wrong! During the night, baby Teddy became very unwell. It turned out that he had contracted meningitis. Julia didn't, in fact, return to London the next day, and when she did, it was without Teddy, who is buried in the family plot in Carlow. She wistfully said as she was leaving:

'That's the last time you'll ever read the cards for me, Maggie.'

And it was.

Ada, the third stepsister, spent many years working in Julia's pubs in London, eventually moving back to live in a flat in Dublin. She was extremely religious and went to different sodalities and novenas every night of the week. She never married, but had a large circle of friends whom she relied on.

Since Gertie was the only child of her mother's second marriage and her parents were getting elderly, she was frequently summoned home to Brown Street to look after the business when the need arose. She often told the story that on one visit home during the War of Independence, which raged from 1919 to 1921, she was approached by an IRA sympathiser to go to the assistance of three men who had been arrested and were being held at the barracks. As a well-educated, respectable young woman, she was well-positioned to act as an intermediary. She was told that they hadn't yet been searched and that they had in their possession two Mills grenades.

Gertie knew the officer in charge at the barracks and somehow managed to convince him to let her in to see the prisoners. The story goes that she relieved them of the bombs by hiding them under her skirt, then walked right through town to throw them over Graiguecullen bridge, into the river Barrow. When she told this story, she was always at pains to say that the IRA was different at that time, saying: 'Respectable people were in the IRA then!' But it was certainly a brave deed to undertake, and shows Gertie's gutsy determination which was at odds with the expected norms for a privileged young lady.

Gertie's mother, Margaret, was from a family where musical evenings were the norm. Since she grew up with seven girls in her household, suitable young men would be invited to attend and all the girls would sing to impress. While Margaret herself seems to have been more practical than musical, Gertie loved singing and was in the ladies chorus of Carlow Choral Society, which annually presented Gilbert and Sullivan operas in the Town Hall in the first week in May. Although she never played the lead part, she was, according to Mr. Aidan Murray (a teacher and businessman who wrote her obituary in 1982) a star in her own right. He recalled the producer saying:

'Gals, gals! This is not a funeral! Smile, smile! Pretend you are in love with the pirates. Look at Gertie, revelling in every minute of it.'

Gertie's mother suffered with bronchitis on a regular basis and, on another visit home to help out, Gertie noticed a handsome young man passing the house in Brown Street. He was a compositor who was on loan to *The Nationalist* newspaper from his permanent post in *The Observer* in Naas, and was staying locally. She made polite conversation with him on a regular basis, by her own admission arranging to clean the windows as he was passing in order to chat with him. On subsequent visits he decided to stay at her mother's boarding house, prompting one of the other guests to say: 'Isn't it strange how John Perkins gets the biggest dinner every day!' Within months they became engaged. For the second time, one of Russell's boarding house guests would become a husband!

Gertie and John's engagement photograph.

Gertie and John married in the Cathedral of the Assumption, Carlow on June 20th 1927, and set up home on the Dublin Road in Carlow, across the road from the Mercy Convent where she received her secondary education. Gertie continued to help her mother with the business, while John secured permanent employment at *The Nationalist* newspaper. At twenty-seven years old, all was set for Gertie to step out into the world and have a family of her own.

New Life Brings Joy and Sadness

Previously readers learned how Gertie met and married John Perkins, a compositor in the printing department with *The Nationalist and Leinster Times*, in 1927. The young couple made their home on the Dublin Road. Meanwhile, Russell's Registry continued to be run by Gertie's mother Margaret and her stepsister, Maggie, who lived in Brown Street.

Gertie and John's house on Dublin Road was a small, terraced, two-storey dwelling, with the front door opening onto the pavement and a small back garden. The high, stone wall at the rear of the property was the boundary wall of St. Dympna's Hospital, known at the time as 'The Lunatic Asylum.' While it was a far more humble dwelling than Gertie's home in Brown Street, with two reception rooms and two bedrooms, its proximity to her mother and to John's workplace made it a good location.

There was very little private housing in Carlow and rental properties of any kind were in short supply. Theirs was owned by a man called Keogh who owned quite a few houses in the town. Estate agent Major Fitzmaurice, whose office was across the road in Leinster Crescent, was responsible for managing many properties in Carlow at the time, including Mr. Keogh's properties.

The Major is mentioned many times in the George Bernard Shaw letters to Carlow which are featured in the RTE Documentary on One entitled *My Dear Fitzmaurice*. With his impressive moustache, tweed jacket and plus-fours, he lived up to his title and was an imposing presence in the town.

There was a great sense of community on the Dublin Road, although it was very much an urban streetscape. It was the kind of place where the first thing people did every morning was to open the front door and then leave it open all day. Gertie's immediate neighbours were Miss May Bunny to the left and the Meaney family to the right. As the years went on, Gretta Meaney was to become a very close friend and confidante of Gertie's.

Gertie and John were very much in love, and, apart from the fact that he was a very good-looking man, Gertie was attracted to his intelligence and love of reading. He was a master compositor and book-binder and a staunch trade-unionist. In 1928, a year after her marriage, Gertie gave birth to her first child, a daughter, whom she named Dorothy. She had put some thought into that name choice, since a 'Dorothy Perkins' was a very well-known breed of garden rose at the time.

A little over three years later a second child was born – a boy – whom she named John Joseph after her husband and father. Sadly, when he was only ten months old, John Joseph contracted pneumonia and died. It was a devastating blow, and one which took the young couple a long time to get over. For years John couldn't bear to hear anyone singing the Al Jolson song 'Sonny Boy' which was very popular at the time:

Climb upon my knee, Sonny boy,
Though you're only three, Sonny boy,
You've no way of knowing,
There's no way of showing,
What you mean to me, Sonny boy.

One sad story Gertie told was that, a few months after her baby died, a poor woman called to the door looking for food and clothing. While she was giving her a few things she noticed that the baby the woman was carrying in her shawl had no blanket around him.

'I have nothing to wrap him in,' the woman said.

Gertie went to the cupboard and, out of tissue paper, took John Joseph's christening blanket and wrapped the baby in it. A few weeks later the same woman called to the door again and, obviously having forgotten her previous visit, showed Gertie the baby and asked for something to wrap him in. It broke her heart to think that the blanket had either been discarded or sold.

Gertie's father, whom she was very close to, died a few months before John Joseph and, a little over three years later her mother, Margaret, also died, just before Gertie gave birth to her second daughter, whom she called Margaret. All these losses, one after the other, must have had a profound effect on Gertie. However, due to her private nature, she kept a lot of it to herself, sharing her burden only with family and close friends.

After her mother's death, Gertie's stepsister, Maggie, continued the employment agency, boarding house and hackney business. There is a notable difference in the tone of the ads during this period. They are shorter and lack the ostentatious formality of Gertie's mother. One example is:

Russell's Registry, Carlow, require immediately, Cooks, Generals; Kitchen-maids; also men servants.

Another stated bluntly:

Working housekeeper, middle aged, seeks situation to men, excellent references. Apply, Russell's Registry.

Maggie was assisted at this stage by her husband, Jim Ferris, whom she married in 1929, aged thirty-nine. Having married late, she and Jim had no children. However, the boarding house in Brown Street continued to be a hub of activity with both long-term and short-term guests.

One interesting guest was known to one and all as 'Miss Graniels' – a mysterious elderly lady who dressed all in black and didn't mix with the other guests, preferring to stay in her room. She had a large travelling suitcase which held treasures in the form of glamorous sequinned dresses and ball-gowns which she occasionally allowed Maggie's nieces to try on.

Unfortunately, Maggie's health began to deteriorate during the 1930s which limited the time she could spend on the employment agency and, in 1944 she died, aged fifty-four. Her husband, Jim Ferris, continued to live in Brown Street, running the boarding house and hackney service. He subsequently remarried and reared his family there. At this time Gertie took over the running of Russell's Registry, relocating it to her home on the Dublin Road.

Dublin Road with the gates of the Mercy Convent – the arrow indicates the position of Gertie's house.

By this time Gertie had a lot on her plate. She had two daughters, Dorothy and Margaret, to look after and a husband with such a serious heart condition that he could die at any moment. He worked diligently through his illness, but Gertie worried endlessly about him. However, it was a point of honour with her to keep her mother's memory alive and also a valuable means of earning some money, which was in short supply.

Like her mother before her, Gertie put her ingenuity to work at times of adversity. Although her house on Dublin Road was small, the parlour was rearranged to receive clients. Her daughter Margaret recalls that there was a routine that even she, aged only around twelve, would have to go through should someone call. If Gertie was out, Margaret was to hold on to any clients until she got back. She would invite the person into the parlour, take down all their details, previous employment etc. This was all written into a ledger. She would then explain that the fee was half a crown. If they were unwilling to pay, she would close the book and stand up to let them out saying nothing could be done for them. This usually had the desired outcome and she would skip down the path to meet her mother, delighted to have contributed to the family income.

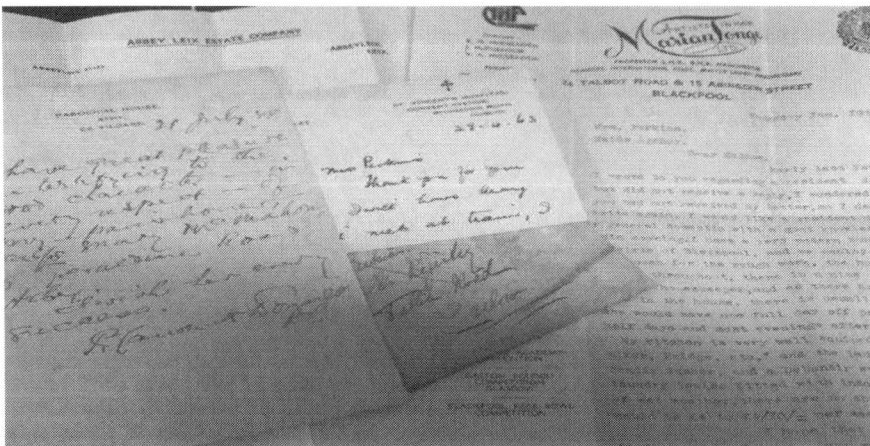

A selection of Gertie's correspondence

Gertie began advertising for the agency in 1944 and her ads had all the grandeur of her mother, and more besides. It was an advantage that, since John worked in the printing department of *The Nationalist* newspaper, the charge for placing the ads was waived so she didn't need to be economical with her words. One of her first ads read:

Employers, write or call to an old established Registry, for your maids, etc. Courtesy and efficiency. Russell's Registry, Dublin Road, Carlow.

However, at this time, John's poor health cast a huge shadow over every aspect of their lives and it was a few years later before she could dedicate herself to the business properly.

When the Parlour Became the Office

It was the 1940s and, at this time in Ireland, the domestic service industry was thriving. Russell's Registry advertised both locally and nationally and Gertie had clients countrywide, as well as some in England. Employers would contact her with their requirements for maids, stable-hands and similar workers and the agency would then place someone from their books with them. A fee was paid by both parties.

It was essential to have references, and they were carefully scrutinised by Gertie, who had a skilled eye for what was omitted as well as what was written. She was known to challenge her daughters who helped her in the business, by showing them a reference and asking their opinion on it. If they said it was a good reference, she would say, 'Look at it again. Look for what's missing.' Very often it was the word 'honest' she was referring to, and she'd remark, 'Not worth the paper it's written on!'

In the Ireland of the time, a reference from the Parish Priest or Rector was a must. The clergy must have been inundated with requests for letters of recommendation, judging by Gertie's correspondence. The focus of these letters was often more on the status of the family in the community than on the individual themselves, and each was stamped by an embossing press with the unique parish seal of authentication. Some of the gentry had similar seals.

Here are some samples of references which were found in Gertie's effects and date back to the 1940s (the names of the employees in each case have been altered to Mona Murphy – not a real name.)

Roseneath,

November 10th, 1945

I have known Mona Murphy since her early childhood, and can vouch for her being a thoroughly good, conscientious girl in every way.

She has often been employed by me as a domestic keep and proved herself to be most capable and hardworking – very kind and helpful.

She is an excellent cook and understands the care and management of children. I shall be pleased at any time to answer any questions on her behalf.

Mrs. C O'Connor

Another, from the Parochial House, Rathoe, in 1944, reads:

July 1949

Miss Mona Murphy – a native of this parish – is personally known to me for almost twenty years. She bears an excellent character and reputation and belongs to a decent family.

I believe too, that she is highly qualified in cooking and housekeeping.

Rev. J. Dunne

Gertie placed many housemaids and servants in the Royal Hotel, Carlow and had numerous references from this source, such as the following:

Royal Hotel, Carlow

4/6/1940

Mona Murphy has been a housemaid at the above hotel for a period of three months – March 1940 to June 1940. She is a quiet, respectable girl, and understood her duties as housemaid and was very attentive to her work. She is strictly honest.

She leaves work at her own request and, I understand, is anxious to take a situation in a private house. All wages and insurance cards stamped to date.

N. Dowling (Manageress)

The Royal Hotel on Dublin Street

The young girl in the following reference sounds like a true gem, and one can only imagine what family commitments must have pressurised her into giving up her employment.

Tullow, Co. Carlow,

October 4th, 1944

I wish to state that Mona Murphy was in my employment for three years. I was <u>very</u> sorry to lose her. She always proved herself a faithful, honest and excellent servant. At housekeeping, cooking, laundry, dairy and poultry, she knows the job perfectly, and above all, she is scrupulously clean and tidy. She is thoroughly good and steady in every way.

In time of illness especially, has she shown her readiness and willingness to work and help in every way. Owing to her brother being recently married she does not intend to take up any more temporary work.

Mrs. O'Leary

At this time, in her personal life, Gertie was struggling. Her husband, although a very ill man, never missed a day at work. Money was tight and she was rearing two young daughters. Her neighbour, Gretta Meaney, was one of the only people Gertie confided in, knowing that private matters would go no further. They would talk over a cup of tea in each other's kitchens and support each other in difficult times.

There were three shops on the Dublin Road – two called 'Whelans', although unrelated, and one known as 'Mrs. Price's'. Gertie's favourite was the latter and she went there on a daily basis, as she and Mrs. Price were kindred spirits. Both of them had been governesses in their youth and enjoyed talking about books and opera. Mrs. Price, whose shop sold all the essential groceries, as well as a selection of cakes and sweets, was well-spoken and ladylike, qualities greatly admired by Gertie.

Opposite Gertie's house stood four tall, imposing, three-storey houses; Leinster Crescent. One was in flats, with the ground floor being occupied by ex-British Army Major Fitzmaurice to whom Gertie paid her weekly rent. Gertie would send one of her daughters with the rent rather than bring it herself, as she resented appearing subservient to anyone. Mrs. 'Doctor' O'Donohue (who was referred to as such although her doctor husband had been dead for years) and Mrs Murphy lived side by side, and finally there was Miss McGovern. She was a primary teacher who, in her forties, became Mrs. Smyth. Gertie respected her, describing her as 'a lady.'

Dublin Road in the direction of the Court House – Gertie's house would have been behind the camera, but was similar to these two-storey houses.

Right next to Leinster Crescent was the Mercy Convent and St. Leo's Secondary School for girls. This was a boarding and day school of some standing and, since it was her *alma mater*, Gertie knew all the nuns by name. She had one good friend there, Sr. Eithne, who was confined to a wicker wheelchair and lived in a separate building in the school grounds. She was an English lady, and she and Gertie developed a friendship which lasted for years.

Life in the Perkins household was a low-key affair. Family outings consisted of long walks together or trips to the cinema. Gertie and John had a harmonious relationship, although arguments did occur since they were both quite hot-headed. Margaret remembers that all rows ended with John extending his hand and saying, 'Sorry Gert,' to which Gertie would look long-suffering, although on many occasions she was the one who had escalated the argument.

John came home from work at 1pm each day and, like most families at the time, they ate their dinner at that time and had tea at six. When his dinner was over, John would stand up and kiss Gertie on the cheek before he left. Only once did he stay a night with his family in Naas, announcing the next day that in future he would only visit for a few hours but wouldn't stay away from Gertie again.

A neighbour, Martin Doogue, remembers Gertie at this time as a stylish woman who would never leave the house without her hat and make-up. He described her as 'elegance personified!' She was very conscious of her appearance at all times and, although occasionally items were surreptitiously sent to the pawn shop to supplement the family income, she never let the side down publicly.

Once, Gertie had an ingenious idea to make some extra money. There was a small plot of wasteland close to their house where men would leave their bicycles when they went to a football match. A man looked after the bikes using a ticket system. There was a big match coming up and Gertie made copious amounts of sandwiches with a view to selling them through a hatch in their hallway, which had in previous years been a shop. When all the sandwiches were ready, the match was cancelled! Margaret remembers that they and the neighbours were eating the sandwiches for days. While this was a catastrophe at the time, it became a funny story that was told and retold for years.

Gertie in the late 1940s

Hard Climb Back from Heartache

Gertie was a woman of honour – a true and loyal friend who expected the same standards from others. If she wanted to make sure someone was telling her the truth she would say, 'Say, on your word of honour,' believing that no one would lie having said those words. She insisted that all the family show respect for people, no matter what their circumstances, and expected the same in return.

Gertie's daughters, Dorothy and Margaret

In the 1940s, Gertie's daughter Dorothy came into the spotlight both locally and nationally, since her striking good looks resulted in her winning beauty contests which were very much in vogue at the time. She represented Carlow at the 'Dawn Beauty' competition in the Metropole Hotel in Dublin three years in a row. This was the precursor to the 'Miss Ireland' competition.

Dorothy was tall and elegant with jet black hair and cupid's bow lips and had many potential suitors. However, John was a very strict and principled father who guarded his daughters vehemently. He insisted on rules and curfews, while Gertie was a little more lenient. She would allow Dorothy and Margaret to listen to Radio Luxembourg on the nights their father worked late, as long as they promised to be in bed before he arrived home. He was very proud of Dorothy and, in truth, believed nobody was good enough for her.

Margaret Perkins, my mother, who was always known within the family as 'Tommy' because of her boyish exuberance, was born in October 1935. She and Dorothy couldn't have been more different, with Dorothy being diligent and conscientious, while Margaret was more of a rule-breaker. However, as sisters they were inseparable, a friendship that flourished throughout their entire lives, until Dorothy's death in 2019.

A common request Gertie made of her daughters in the late '40s was to go and meet their father coming from work, for fear his heart would fail and he might collapse in the street. Margaret was in her early teens at this stage and painfully aware of the anxiety around her father's health. Dorothy was a young lady in her early twenties who had begun working as a hairdresser in Corr's of Tullow Street.

One Sunday afternoon in 1950 he went for his afternoon nap and, when Margaret went to call him, she found him unresponsive with an open P.G. Wodehouse book beside him. She had just turned fifteen. Dorothy was twenty-two. Gertie wasn't at home, so Dorothy stayed with her father while Margaret ran to Dublin Street to get Dr. Larry Doyle. Sadly, it was too late. Gertie came running into the house a few minutes later to be told by Doctor Doyle, 'He died instantaneously.' Words never to be forgotten. For his lifetime companion, Gertie, her worst fear had become a reality and life would never be the same again.

Gertie and John shortly before his death.

In the aftermath, Gertie leaned heavily on her neighbour and confidante, Gretta Meaney. The Meaneys had four children, three boys and a girl. Once a month Gertie and Gretta walked to a 'Third Order' religious ceremony in Graiguecullen church on the other side of the river. On one of these walks, Gertie confided in Gretta that she was running dangerously short of money and that she was going to pray for help. She wouldn't have told this to anyone else.

Amazingly, Gertie's prayers were answered! In a week or two she got a letter in the post to say she had won two hundred and fifty pounds in the Sunday Independent 'Spot the Ball' competition. Every week an action picture of a soccer match was printed with players looking in different directions. The ball was omitted and the entrant had to place an x where they thought the ball should be. Gertie would not have been *au fait* with soccer, but using her powers of logic, not to mention divine intervention, she won! This was a large sum of money at the time and Gertie certainly saw it as a godsend.

Following John's death, Gertie's grief caused her to neglect the agency somewhat. Photos of Gertie around this time show a haggard, sickly lady without her characteristic style. Grief wasn't something that was overtly discussed, manifesting itself mostly in Gertie as anxiety and sleeplessness. During this period the family moved into a new house on MacGamhna Road, as their house on Dublin Road was to be demolished.

This was a time of tumultuous change for all of them and, for a period of time, Dorothy and Margaret's biggest job was looking after their mother. The employment agency was re-established in one of the two reception rooms, and gradually, by throwing herself into the business, Gertie began to rebuild her life. Like her mother before her, she took in two boarders and set her shoulder to the wheel again, and by 1955 the agency was back on its feet and Russell's Registry lived on.

In addition to her usual placing of maids and stable-hands, Gertie received an interesting letter from San Sebastian in Spain at this time. It was from an elderly lady, originally from Carlow town, who had left with her sister many years before. The purpose of the correspondence was to find a placement for a young man to improve his English as he intended to move to Canada or Australia. While she is effusive in her praise for the kindly letter she received from Gertie, she is anything but complimentary about the Carlow she left behind.

An excerpt reads:

I really have no kind remembrance of Carlow, neither of nuns, priests or people, nor school days. Too much snobbism, too much pride. Well God be with them all and bless them, they never did anything for us.

She goes on to explain that her mother passed away leaving her father with ten children to raise on his own and that no one came to his help.

They let us drop altogether from the time of Mamma's death. We got poor and from Pembroke came to a small house in Burrin Street and then to rooms in Brown Street. Nobody ever looked at us again.

She did, however, have fond memories of one Carlow business family – the Gough's from Tullow Street.

I was very fond of dear Mrs. Robert Gough and family. They were very kind to me. I know the parents are dead, but Mary Joe and Kathleen may be still in business – they were good girls. I wonder will they be as nice as their parents or have they become snobbish?

Gough's drapery shop, at 139 Tullow Street, was run by Mrs. Robert Gough and then by her daughters right up to the 1970s, when it was sold to Good's Hardware Store.

In signing off, this lady concluded her letter with:

You'll think me a terrible person to say all this, but with regard to us, it's true. Thank you so much for writing a friendly letter instead of a stiff, business one, and do please write again…. Kindest regards and good luck to you. God bless you.

Gertie was a prolific letter writer. Her office desk was neatly laid out with Basildon Bond writing paper and envelopes, a letter-opener, the ledger in which she took down client's details and a date-stamp. Although her handwriting was uneven, the content and grammar of each sentence was impeccable and anything less would be scrapped. Her headed paper, after the death of her husband, continued to describe the proprietress as 'Mrs. J. Perkins', keeping his memory alive, and in deference to her mother, she always included the line 'Estd. 1900.'

Gertie began to expand the business at this time, establishing links with large institutions and supplying staff for them. One such client was Butlins Holiday Centre in County Meath. This new and exciting holiday centre, opened in 1948, was the first of its kind outside the UK and Gertie was responsible for sending many Carlow people for seasonal work there. Some described this period as being the 'time of their lives.'

The Good, the Bold and the Brazen!

After her husband John Perkins' death, there followed a very low time in Gertie's life, in which she was grief-stricken and found it very hard to adjust to her new reality. Her daughters, Dorothy and Margaret, were twenty-two and fifteen years old respectively, and it was incumbent on Gertie now to be the bread-winner and to ensure Russell's Registry was a viable enterprise.

So, over the following few years, in her early fifties, Gertie became Mrs. Perkins – survivor. Her future was entirely in her own hands. Her two daughters were on the cusp of adulthood and beginning to make lives for themselves. By necessity she needed to build a business that would challenge her mentally as well as support her financially. This she did with aplomb. The next twenty-five years would be filled with intriguing encounters, fascinating letters and interesting connections which illuminate a bygone time in Irish social history. And at the centre of it all was the 'Ubiquitous Gertie.'

In 1955, Gertie's daughter, Dorothy married John McKinley, a native of Warrenpoint in County Down. The wedding was held in Carlow Cathedral and the report in *The Nationalist* of August 6th 1955 states:

The bride, who was given away by Mr. William Grey, wore a ballet length gown of white Chantilly lace over taffeta, with a wreath and finger-tip veil of white tulle. She carried a bouquet of red carnations.

Nineteen-year-old Margaret was the bridesmaid and the photographs show a very proud Gertie standing beside her two resplendent adult daughters.

Dorothy, Margaret and Gertie at Dorothy's wedding in 1955

At this time, Gertie's daughter Margaret still lived at home with her, having begun her career in *The Nationalist* newspaper as the first female reporter. Dorothy began her married life living only a stone's throw from the family home in Green Lane. A new chapter was opening up for Gertie and, before the 1950s were out, she would become the proud grandmother to Dorothy's two children, Carol and Barry.

Being interviewed for a position by Gertie was not for the faint-hearted. There was an air of the Reverend Mother about how she conducted business, and clients – mostly young women – were told in no uncertain terms how they were expected to conduct themselves.

'You're going to a quality house', she would say, 'and I expect quality behaviour!'

'Quality behaviour' mostly involved deference – addressing people by their correct titles, not being over-familiar, having impeccable table manners and never being loud or raucous.

Similarly, if Gertie felt that a potential employer was being less than respectful to her, she had her own way of dealing with that. She would make them wait, look them in the eye and say:

'It doesn't suit me to deal with your requirements at the moment!'

The more arrogant or demanding a person was, the longer they would wait. She was also known to challenge employers if she heard they were overworking the staff she sent them. While not a tall woman, the way she commanded a room and the angle of her chin, made her gargantuan in other ways.

One not so satisfied customer was a lady in Rathmines in Dublin. She wrote in 1947 as follows:

Just a hurried note to tell you I have had a fearful time with Mona Murphy (not her real name) – she is at present in Mountjoy Jail. She had the full of her case of my clothes – my daughter's and son's – and, under the mattress, foodstuffs etc. She had ransacked everywhere, including my wardrobe, and that was locked.

I sent my son up to her former employer. She had received just that morning from Mona Murphy's mother, a parcel of clothes that she had written to be returned or else to put the police on her. She examined Mona's case and found numerous things of hers – so she is also charging her. I never met a more brazen girl!

It's unclear what became of Mona Murphy, but the employer signed off with:

I was terribly upset. Would you please return my fee!

A sting in the tail that would undoubtedly have upset Gertie.

On the contrary, a Mary Sweeney produced two glowing references which must have impressed Gertie in 1949. They are from 'Stella Maris' Nursing Home in Earlsfort Terrace and St. Jarlath's Nursing Home in Herbert Street in Dublin. Both describe her as a clean, honest girl – in one, honest is even underlined! She was also 'agreeable, obliging and willing' and left of her own free will. One can only assume that Gertie had no difficulty in placing Mary.

In the same year, a lady from Belgrave Road in Dublin recommended a Mary McMahon very highly indeed:

She is absolutely reliable, and understands her duties thoroughly. She is an early riser, very punctual, clean in her personal habits, very economical and careful of objects in her charge – anyone employing her will be making no mistake!

It's hard to imagine what Gertie would have made of the two references produced by Ann Doyle (not her real name) in 1954. One from her Parish Priest begins with the line:

I do not know Ann Doyle……..However I have made enquiries and I feel I can safely give her a good recommendation. She has received the usual

Primary education in the National School, and later attended the Secondary School conducted by the nuns in Goresbridge. Signed... P Nolan P.P.

The one from the nuns was even more non-committal, if that is possible:

Miss Ann Doyle was a day pupil in this Secondary School for two years. She was docile and obedient and made progress in her studies compatible with her intellectual ability.

Poor Ann! One hopes life turned out well for her.

In 1958 Gertie went abroad for the first and only time in her life. While she had worked in London as a young lady, she never travelled any farther and her first passport was issued just in time for her to go on pilgrimage to Lourdes with her daughter, Margaret. They travelled with Shannon Travel, Dublin and were accommodated with the Limerick Diocesan Pilgrimage led by none other than Father Eamon Casey (later to become Bishop!)

In those days pilgrimages were penance in themselves. There were no direct flights or luxury coaches. Gertie and Margaret set sail from Dun Laoghaire to Holyhead on Tuesday September 16th on the overnight sailing, then travelled by train to Folkestone and by boat to Boulogne. From there they took a train to Gare du Nord in Paris where they spent their second night. They arrived in Lourdes station at 10pm on the night of the 18th. Four days were spent in Lourdes in the appropriately named 'Irelande' hotel, before making the gruelling return journey.

The crossing on the way home was very rough and almost everyone was sick. But not Gertie! She spent the voyage on her feet, going up and downstairs, bringing glasses of water to her fellow pilgrims. Despite the hardship of travel, both Gertie and Margaret had very fond memories of their trip to Lourdes. It was the closest they had ever been to spending time together in a carefree way and both were struck by the faith of the pilgrims and the kindness shown to the very ill.

As is usual they brought home blessed religious medals and Holy Water, which was distributed among their neighbours and friends. These were treasured items. However, the only memento I remember in Gertie's house was a curious one, probably bought for practical rather than religious purposes. It was a travel cup with Lourdes written on the side, but what made it fascinating to my childish eyes was that it was collapsible. Made up of different sized rings which, when pulled up, fitted together perfectly, it held liquid so not a drop was spilled. Magic!

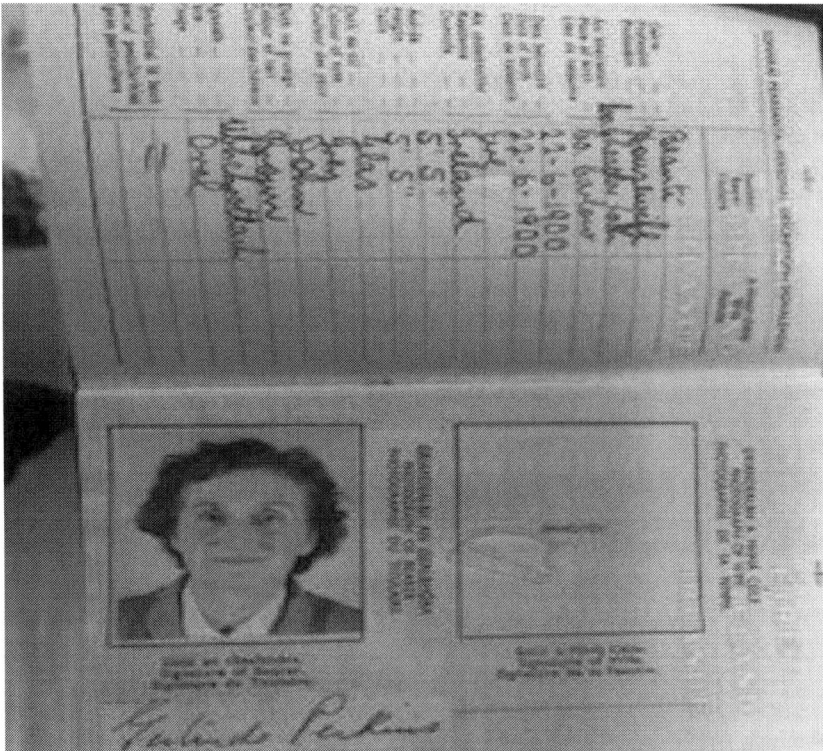

Gertie's first and only passport, issued in 1958

So the fifties came to a close for Gertie in a more positive way. After the turmoil of losing her husband, she had managed to rebuild her life. Her family had extended to include a son-in-law and grandchildren and, with her daughter, Margaret, now financially secure, they could enjoy life in a new way. Running Russell's Registry was now not so much a necessity as something which she enjoyed, and which gave her life purpose. The role suited her and she was clearly successful in it.

Russell's Registry Thriving into the Sixties

The 1950s came to a close with Gertie living with her daughter Margaret in MacGamhna Road. Her daughter, Dorothy, was now married and living close by with her husband, John, and Gertie's two grandchildren, Carol and Barry. Gertie took an active role in looking after her grandchildren and teaching them the rudiments of good manners and table etiquette – topics close to her heart!

Gertie ran Russell's Registry from one of her downstairs rooms – a room she referred to as 'The Office'. After a short while, she had a phone installed. It was a black payphone with Buttons A and B and, on this, she conducted her business. She always had a ready supply of coins nearby, since, especially on a long-distance call, you had to be ready to insert coins as soon as the operator asked, or you would be cut off. However, Gertie preferred meeting people face to face, and most of her clients attended by appointment.

While, thankfully, most of her clients were well-placed and happy, there were always some exceptions. In 1961 Gertie was provided with a copy of two letters – one from the mother of a servant from Carlow to her employer and the other from the girl's employer in Dublin. The mother's letter goes as follows:

Dear Mrs. Murphy,

A line to say Kathleen got home safe on Sunday, T.G, but I need not tell you we were greatly shocked to see how thin she got. She must have had a lot of work to do since she was at home at Easter. She was grand then, but a changed girl – very pale. But please God, when she is at home for a few days she will pull up again.

... You treated her badly. You gave her no holiday money and she's entitled to a week after seven months. Also, I never thought for a moment you were stopping (money) for her stamps out of her wages as Mrs. Perkins said you would give her £3 a week and a rise after a while.

... I do hope you will send her week's pay for her holidays. If she does not like England she may be home again and you might like to have her back and could you expect her to go if you don't treat her properly?

... Hope there will be no offence.

Yours sincerely, Bernie Brennan (not her real name)

This letter and the reply were sent to Gertie. It is lengthy and, clearly, Mrs. Murphy in Stillorgan was not happy! An extract here sums it up:

I'm afraid I cannot fail to resent your remarks that Kathleen was badly treated. She was treated as one of the family, taken for drives and to the cinema, and allowed to watch television with us. I also gave a wireless set for her own use and this may account for her paleness; she spent many lovely evenings up in her room listening in and writing letters, although I did my best to encourage her to go out in the sunshine. In addition to her two half days each week she was free to go out every evening had she chosen. Your letter has taught me one thing, which is never to bother again about the entertainment of any girl whom I may have in the house.

Mrs. Murphy was clearly in high dudgeon! She signs off rather haughtily:

I accept your apology for the tone of your letter but, as I said at the beginning, you were ill-advised to write so hurriedly.

However, for all her apparent confidence, Mrs. Murphy was clearly worried that Gertie would think badly of her. In her letter to Gertie she says:

You may wonder why I should send these letters to you but, as Mrs. Brennan's letter expresses such dissatisfaction of my treatment of her daughter...it is quite probable she may approach you on the subject. As it was you who sent Kathleen to us, and in case we may have to call upon you again, I would like you to know that we are not the kind of ogres that Mrs. Brennan seems to think and Kathleen was not treated as a little slavey of the last century!

One would love to have been a fly on the wall when Gertie received these letters. Unfortunately, her response is not available to us, but I think it would be safe to say, she would give the benefit of the doubt to Kathleen, as she was a stickler for fair pay and conditions.

In 1962, Gertie's daughter, Margaret, married fellow journalist Seamus O'Rourke. Again, they would live within the environs of Carlow town in Rathnapish, a short walk from Gertie's house. Within three years, Gertie had two more grandchildren, Ruth and I. Sadly two boys would follow, John and Fiacc, who both died shortly after birth. Throughout the '60s Gertie was a great support to Margaret in both the good and bad times, and since she had experienced the death of her own infant son, John Joseph, years before, she understood the grief of these losses. Another grandchild, Jane, followed in the early '70s.

This was a time of loyalty in business in Carlow town and Gertie was a staunch supporter of several local establishments. Her weekly shopping was done in the L&N, while she also ran a 'book' with Mary Teresa Kelly, both in Tullow Street. Mary Kelly became a family friend and there were presents exchanged at Christmas and on special occasions. Gertie's shopping-list from Mary included Consulate cigarettes, a quarter pound of biscuits, *The Irish*

Press, Bob's Your Uncle ticket and fruit, as well as sugar and Lyons tea. Mary would be paid at the end of the month and would always give a gift of sweets or chocolate on pay day. Both of Gertie's daughters continued the tradition of shopping at Mary Kelly's.

Gertie and Margaret at Margaret's wedding in 1962

Gertie's doctor was Dr. Larry Doyle and then his son, Dr. Brendan Doyle senior. She frequented Michael White's pharmacy and occasionally Corless's. Her skirts were made by Leslie Williams in St. Killian's crescent and her shoes mended by Charlie Lewis in Dublin Street. Gertie was a familiar figure to many in town on shopping day with her 'Sunday-go-to-meeting-hat' and net bag. On Sundays and some weekdays, she sat in the right-hand aisle of the Cathedral – and for Mass she always wore her fur necklet.

Gertie with her grandchildren, Barry and Carol, in Butlins in the '60's

In the Sixties Russell's Registry was in its heyday under Gertie's command. She was now receiving correspondence from many parts of Ireland and some from abroad. Locally she was known as the lady who could find you a good job. An interesting letter she received from Blackpool at the time reads as follows:

Mrs. Perkins. Maids Agency!

I would like a resident housekeeper or general domestic with a good knowledge of plain cooking. I have a very modern bungalow on the outskirts of Blackpool, and we employ a part-time charwoman for the rough work....

My kitchen is very well-equipped, Kenwood food mixer, fridge etc, and the laundry room has a Bendix Washer, and a Debonair spin-drier.

Well, what more could anyone ask for! To further impress, Mrs. McCullough adds:

The laundry is also fitted with indoor drying in case of wet weather. There are no children and the wage would be £4 to £4/10 per week.

I don't know who Gertie suited to this paragon of modernity, but I wonder would it have suited the lady who wrote the following letter of application:

Dear Mrs. Perkins,

I rang you last night but I couldn't hear you on the phone. I was just asking you if you could get me into a private house or a guest house where I wouldn't have to cook or mind children as I don't like children. So, I hope you can get me something very soon.

Yours Sincerely,

Mona Murphy (not her real name)

No work and no children! Tricky!

Sometimes Gertie's work wasn't easy! With a reference like the following from a curate in Bagenalstown, it certainly didn't help:

To whom it may concern,

I wish to state that I know both the parents and children of this family for about twelve years and I can say that they are quite good parishioners and there is nothing that I can say of adverse criticism against them!

Not exactly a letter to get you into heaven!

Detective Gertie!

Gertie's professionalism ensured she had a broad spectrum of clients on the books at Russell's Registry and she got great satisfaction from matching employees to suitable workplaces. To some people, she became a type of counsellor, providing a confidential listening ear, as well as advice. One thing that really annoyed Gertie was to hear that an employer was treating their employee unfairly or overworking them. And Gertie was certainly not afraid to let her feelings be known.

On one such occasion Gertie noticed that a certain farmer was regularly looking for new farm-hands. At first, she wasn't sure if he was employing them all or whether they weren't staying long. But then one of the young men came to see her and told her that conditions were poor and that he had left. So, Gertie, not being a driver herself, hired a car to bring her to the farmyard unannounced!

You can imagine the farmer's surprise to see Gertie emerging from a car in his yard. He welcomed her and brought her into the house. During the conversation Gertie brought up the matter of the staff turnover rate, but the farmer explained it away by saying: 'You know young lads nowadays – they don't stay at anything for long.'

Unphased, Gertie asked if he would mind showing her where the farm-hands stayed at night. He pointed to an outbuilding, but didn't volunteer to show her any further. Slowly Gertie walked over and opened the door. Inside were four bunk-beds, with straw instead of mattresses and there was no light or heating.

'I think I can see why they don't stay long,' she said.

'No, no, Mrs. Perkins, this is not permanent. I'm getting another place done up and they'll be staying there.'

Gertie gave him one of her steely looks and said:

'When you have it done up, contact me and I'll come out and see it. Until then, don't bother me again. Good day.'

And she closed the car door firmly.

A very tragic story Gertie told was of a young man from the midlands who came to see her one day in Russell's Registry's early days on the Dublin Road. She had suited him with a summer job previously, but hadn't seen him for a few years. He said he needed a job urgently and explained that he had been away in a seminary but had decided to leave. Gertie asked if he would not consider working on his own father's farm, but he shook his head sadly.

He told her that when he left the seminary he had made his way home. On approaching the gate he heard his father's voice:

'Don't take another step and don't put your hand on that gate. I have a gun on you. Never come back here again.'

Gertie was touched by this story and, even as an old lady, talked about how her heart went out to this young man.

As a matter of urgency, she placed him in an agricultural college where she had contacts and never had to place him again, as his diligence and hard work meant that it became for him a highly successful career.

In the 1960s, Gertie's fame had spread far and wide and she was placing young people from Carlow and the surrounding areas in far-flung places. The following is a letter which must surely have been life-changing for some young local girl:

Dear Mrs. Perkins,

I am writing to enquire about the possibility of finding a girl through your agency who would like to come to the United States to work in my home. We would like to find someone who is fond of children and between twenty and forty years old. Some experience in housework is preferred, but not absolutely necessary. The wage is $250 per month with one and a half days off each week – own room with television.

We have seven children. The youngest is one and the eldest is seventeen. I have cleaning help one day a week and send out some of the ironing. We live in an area where there are other Irish girls with whom she can become acquainted, and we live just nineteen miles from Chicago with fine train transportation.

The girl would have two hours off each afternoon as I expect her to help through dinner hour. On family occasions we would expect her to live as part of the family. Sincerely hope to hear from you soon. Mrs. Darby, Illinois

Gertie's extended family was very small, two of her three sisters having no children. In fact, after the death of baby Teddy, outlined in a previous instalment, Gertie had only one niece and nephew – Kate and Jackie O'Connor, Julia's children who lived in London. During World War 1, for safety Jackie, aged two, was sent over to live in Brown Street, when Gertie was about sixteen years old. During this period he became like a little brother to her, and they remained close throughout their lives.

Jackie joined the Merchant Navy for a time, but having received an inheritance from his paternal grandmother who owned some public houses in London's West End, he decided to set up a travelling show, as he was an accomplished musician. On one visit to Carlow to see Gertie, he was reputed to have played the piano in the Irishman's Bar one night and the standard of his performance astonished those patrons who heard him.

Jackie was generous to Gertie and always treated her as his favourite aunt. When she moved into MacGamhna Road after the death of her husband John, Jackie visited and bought her a new cooker for the house. He kept up regular correspondence and sometimes sent gift-cheques which were gratefully received.

Gertie's nephew, Jackie O'Connor

Unfortunately, Jackie was too trusting and, while he loved touring Ireland and England with the travelling show, he arrived at Gertie's one day and sadly reported that his agent had relieved him of most of his inheritance. 'I trusted him,' he said. Now all he could do was return to England virtually penniless.

The last Gertie heard from Jackie was in the '60s. By then her sister Julia and brother-in-law John O'Connor had died and her niece, Kate, had never really kept in touch. For a couple of years Gertie waited in hope and watched the post-box expectantly, especially at Christmas, but there was no word from Jackie.

'Jackie O'Connor must be dead,' she said ruefully.

The only way Gertie could find out for sure was to contact the Salvation Army, which she did. Sadly, they turned up no results and Gertie lived the rest of her days wondering what became of him.

Although Gertie turned seventy in nineteen seventy, having been born on the longest day of the year, June 21st, 1900, she showed no sign of slowing down. If anything, she had come into her own in business and was surrounded by her family, which extended to five grandchildren with the birth of Jane in 1973. But then an unfortunate accident changed everything.

One day Gertie was going about her everyday chores as usual. She emerged from her house to do some shopping when suddenly her dog, Rex, ran in front of her, and she fell headlong down the steps in front of her house. Gertie was brought to St. Brigid's hospital – 'The Blue Sisters' as they were known, in Court Place where she received sixty stitches and a skin-graft on her leg, although miraculously, she had broken no bones.

Gertie's recovery took a long time, and she was impatient with it. Not accustomed to sitting down for long periods, she found rest and recuperation very hard. The only thing that kept her mind occupied was dealing with correspondence for Russell's Registry, which was still flowing in. Up to 1976, she was still advertising in *The Nationalist* and occasionally *The Evening Herald*, and placing people countrywide.

Gertie was a wonderful storyteller with a sharp eye for detail. As an old lady she entertained us, her grandchildren, with stories of the Carlow she grew up in, which is one of the reasons I have been able to write these articles. She brought characters to life whom we had never met and places we had never seen. Governey's Boot Factory, the dispute in the Sugar Factory, The Gilbert and Sullivan operas in the Deighton Hall, the singing that came from Bridewell Lane. She made us feel like her Carlow was our Carlow and that its history was something we should treasure and preserve.

Gertie Finally Calls it a Day

Sadly, Russell's Registry eventually came to an end, but remembering it has been a window into an era that no longer exists – an intrinsic part of the rich tapestry of Carlow life for three quarters of a century. At the centre of it all was Gertie Perkins, nee Russell, a woman ahead of her time – a survivor and a trail-blazer. It was with sadness and reluctance that she realised, in 1976, that the employment agency may have to come to an end as she was slowing down and was no longer able for the day to day correspondence.

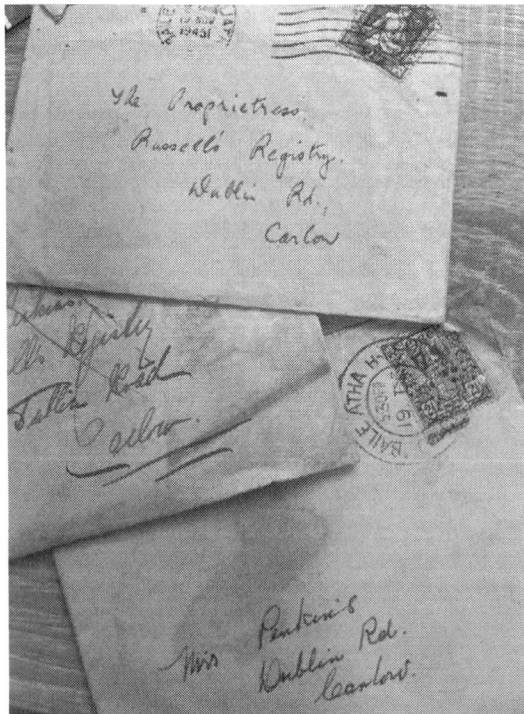

Letters to Russell's Registry

The '70s were an incongruous time in Ireland – in some regards the winds of change were blowing through all that had been taken for granted, while in other ways tradition held strong. It is hard to believe that in the same decade that saw anti-nuclear protests in Carnsore Point and women invading the male dominion of the forty-foot in Sandycove, Gertie received this letter from a man in County Carlow, which sounds like it came straight out of a Dickens' novel.

Dear Madame,

I am looking for a houseman/driver, married or single, who can cook on an Esse or gas cooker, and is a careful driver. I am a bachelor, living alone and leading a very quiet life. There are occasional visitors....

My former man, who has been with me for twenty-two years, has had to retire at only sixty years of age with a serious heart condition. He has told me that I should seek your assistance.

...I should say that this vacancy would be ideal for country people who were interested and entirely trustworthy.'

Equally, in the same year, 1974, this reference was given for a Tom Murphy (not his real name) by the Parish Priest of Baltinglass.

Tom Murphy is one of my parishioners and is well known to me. He comes from a good Catholic family and is a frequent attender at Mass and the sacraments. His moral character is beyond reproach. I would recommend him for a position for which he would have the necessary qualifications.'

I'm not sure if Tom could drive, but if I were Gertie, I think I would consider them a match!

There were a couple of contributing factors to Gertie making the difficult decision to close the registry. One was the changing landscape in employment law in Ireland. Following Ireland's entry into the European Common Market in 1973, a plethora of red tape and bureaucracy was introduced which directly affected Gertie's business. Government forms now had to be filled in for every placement. Advertisements were strictly monitored for equality standards and new occupational safety and health regulations were introduced. Had Gertie been in her heyday, she would have met all these challenges, but at her stage of life, the red tape became overwhelming.

The demise of the big houses which traditionally employed numerous servants and outside workers, as well as modern, labour-saving devices and machinery, meant that Gertie's services were not required as much. While she was still very busy with requests from large colleges and institutions, they too were affected by the changes in employment law and began to move to more mainstream methods of recruiting.

But mostly, and sadly, Gertie became increasingly forgetful and within a few short years, slipped into the abyss of dementia. Unable to keep up with the demands of business, she slipped quietly into private life, cared for by her daughters until she needed hospital care. Gertie ended her days in the Sacred Heart Hospital where she was very content and well looked after. She died on April 26th, 1982, two months short of her eighty-second birthday.

In the first of two tributes written about Gertie in *The Nationalist* in May 1982, Aidan Murray of Murray's Sweet Shop, Dublin Street (recently demolished) and also a Primary School teacher, painted a lovely picture of a vibrant, talented woman. He described in glorious detail a time when the highlight of Carlow's social and cultural life was the annual Gilbert and Sullivan opera, held in the Town Hall.

Nobody under seventy can appreciate the surge of excitement that gripped the town when the huge streamer was erected from P.C. Bergin's premises to the Royal Hotel announcing the name of the new opera.

And of Gertie, he said:

Mrs. Perkins, who remains always in my mind as Gertie Russell, was the last surviving member of the Chorus of Ladies who graced the early productions of Carlow Choral Society... It was as a conversationalist and raconteur that I loved Gertie best. She carried that rare gift of making you feel better for having met her, up to the end. I met her last year for the last time. Despite her advanced age, the voice, the aura of gaiety and happiness were as I remembered them sixty years ago. It was an endless joy to have known her and an honour to be counted among her friends.

The second tribute was written by Odran Seeley, who for many years was Road Safety Officer with Carlow County Council. He focused on Gertie's service, through Russell's Registry, to the people of Carlow and the surrounding areas.

Long before we had government agencies to help the unemployed, the late Mrs. Perkins was filling a vital public need, finding jobs for the young boys and girls who, in the depressed forties and fifties left school at fourteen, the minimum leaving age at that time. She was also, in her own very practical way, Carlow's first career guidance person – assessing, advising, guiding.

This has been borne out in the years since her death by the number of people who have approached the family saying 'Your Granny got me my first job' or words to that effect.

Mr. Seeley went on to say:

Her response to each person who called on her services, whether employer or employee, was highly personal and the profit motive was always secondary to the Christian ethic of helping the distressed, the needy, or the people who, for one reason or another, could be considered unemployable.... She listened to them all, found a solution for many, and never dispatched one of them from her doorstep without a word of advice or comfort.

If Mr. Seeley's tribute had been a reference, it surely would have got Gertie into heaven! He finished rather poetically by saying:

...despite great ability and discernment in her chosen field, she did not die a rich woman. Not in human terms. But those who dealt with her and sensed her interest and understanding have no doubt that her riches were stored in a better place "where neither thief approaches, nor moth destroys."

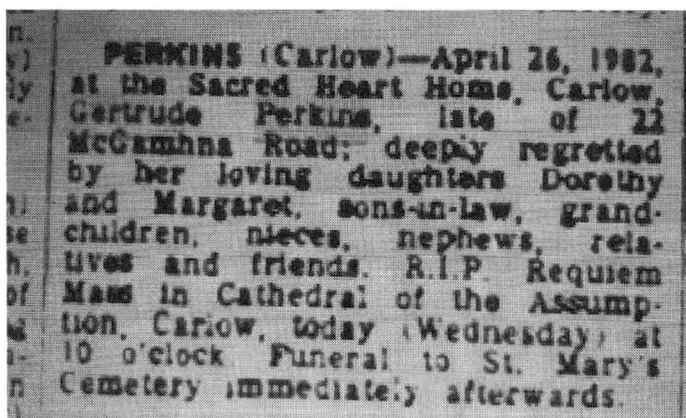

Gertie's Death Notice

In Gertie's final few years, she spoke endlessly about her parents, Margaret and Joseph Russell, with a clarity that defied the scrambled nature of her short-term memory. She told many stories of life in Brown Street in precise detail and of people who were long gone. She found it very difficult to grasp the fact that her parents, in particular her mother, and all those she had loved at that time were gone.

One of the reasons these articles could be compiled is because of Gertie's rich story-telling which, when put together with photographs and documents, allowed the past to be revealed and reconstructed. Even in her latter days, she retained this skill and often entertained her family and close friends to story-telling evenings.

Gertie shortly before she died

One day in the late '70s she ventured out of her daughter's house alone, although in the grip of dementia. While we all searched for her in the neighbourhood and enquired anxiously if anyone had seen her, Gertie had made her way, unfailingly and in double-quick time, to Brown Street. Its occupant at the time, Noel Ferris, recognised Gertie and brought her inside.

His father Jim Ferris's first wife was Gertie's step-sister, Maggie. He kindly gave Gertie a cup of tea and said they were having a great chat when her family came to collect her. When she was driven home, Gertie was completely unaware of the feat she had pulled off by navigating her way from Rathnapish to her old home in Brown Street.

Dismantling Russell's Registry was sad and confining life-changing letters and references to boxes in the attic always seemed somehow incomplete. I'm very glad to have had the opportunity to reopen this chapter of my family's history and the social history of our town. Russell's Registry is a testament to a matriarchy of strong, independent women who used their ingenuity to meet the needs of their community while also earning a living.

Section 4

Carlow Stories

Introduction to 'Carlow Stories'

The following section contains personal stories of my own Carlow memories. One of them entitled 'Mary Kelly's Shop' tells the story of a wonderful shop on Tullow Street whose proprietor endeared herself to many Carlow people. It featured on Sunday Miscellany on RTE in 2021 and can be listened to by using the following link:

https://www.rte.ie/radio/podcasts/21998909-mary-kellys-shop-by-maria-orourke/

Other memories are of going to the outdoor swimming pool in the town park, which later became Shaw Park, and the adventures my friend and I used to have along the way. The piece entitled 'Tomboys' is in the same vein. There is also a memory of an Elocution exam I undertook, which went badly wrong! Another, entitled 'Dining at the Palace' features my grandmother, Gertrude Perkins, who is also the subject of my Russell's Registry series. This story tells of her efforts to teach us, her grandchildren, manners and how she actually led us to believe we might someday meet the queen!

The final two memories are of learning Irish grammar in secondary school in a piece entitled 'Half a declension' and finally a personal memory of my father, Séamus, called 'The Fisherman's Cap.' I hope these stories will amuse and entertain in equal measure. As Maya Angelou said: 'There is no greater agony than bearing an untold story inside you.' May my stories inspire you to write stories of your own.

Mary Kelly's Shop

On the last Friday of every month my mother paid Mary Kelly. I only remember that because of the brown paper bag with crisps and chocolate she sent home for us children on pay day. Cadbury's Dairy Milk, Tayto and a can of Fanta orange each – we didn't even have to share them.

My mother always said the same thing:

'I don't know how that woman makes any profit in her shop. She's way too generous. I'll have to ask her to stop.'

'No!' we wailed. 'Mammy, don't!'

The viability of Mary Kelly's shop was no concern of ours.

Inherited from her mother before her, Mary Kelly's shop was always painted red. The display windows on either side of the door were rearranged regularly – selection boxes and biscuit tins at Christmas, pyramids of Easter eggs during Lent, and Halloween masks in October. There were yellow and red streamers of plastic so that you couldn't see through to the shop from the road, and when Mary was decorating the window, all you could see was her disembodied arm arranging this season's treats.

I never saw Mary Kelly outside of her shop, although I believe she went to 7.30 Mass every morning, returning just in time to sell cigarettes to the men on their way to work in the Sugar Factory. She ran a 'book' for my grandmother, my mother and my aunt, and for countless other Carlow people, mostly women.

The entries were written in a sort of code that only Mary and her customer understood. Sl P was a sliced pan, 10 cigs could mean Silk Cut Red in the case of my mother, Consulate for Granny or Silk Cut Purple for my aunt. Each day, more was added, until a line was drawn at the end to signify payment. My grandmother's last bill came to eight pounds, four shillings and six pence.

Stepping into Mary's shop, a bell rang as the door shut behind you. The counter ran round three sides of the shop with the door into the house directly in front of you on entry. It was from here that Mary would appear, calling, 'Coming, coming,' as she padded into the shop in her house coat and flat shoes, often with a hair-net covering her pink rollers. The house, or what you could see of it through the doorway, looked like the set from a play, with red velour chairs facing a fireplace topped with a ticking clock and a swirly brown carpet.

I remember, as a small child, hearing Mary discuss the new decimal currency that was coming in to replace pounds, shillings and pence. She was holding the orange information leaflet in her hand, saying:

'How will I remember it? I'll never get used to it.'

But get used to it she did, except for the milk. I remember being sent in to get the messages one day shortly afterwards. I had a list, which Mary duly transferred to 'the book.' She muttered to herself as she walked around behind the counter, picking up tea-bags and butter, before turning to me and asking:

'Your Mammy wants milk – did she say you were to get a large litre or a small litre?'

If we were home sick from school, and Mam popped in for a bottle of Lucozade, Mary would reach up to where the Lucky Bags were hanging on a kind of clothes-line over her head. 'Bring this home to the poor child,' she'd say, and the 'poor child' would be ecstatic to unfold the gummed top of the magical, mystery bag containing anything from a lollipop to a tiny yo-yo, a whistle and a bag of jellies.

Sometimes Mary Kelly's sister was visiting and, as soon as we would arrive into the shop, she'd say:

'Hold on, hold on, till I get you a few sweets.'

Mam would say, 'not at all,' despite the glares we shot at her, but Mary's sister wasn't deterred. She'd run around behind the counter to the side that had jars of sweets and bars of chocolate and, reaching for the bullseyes or gobstoppers, she'd say, 'Catch!' before rolling them one by one across the counter. Then, from both sides of the shop in stereo, the two sisters would marvel at how tall we'd got, how like our granny or our cousins we were and what lovely clothes we were wearing.

Mary Kelly's is boarded up now. The big supermarkets opened, the Sugar Factory closed and Mary retreated into old age to her silent sitting room, waiting for another bell to ring. But when she finally left us, it wasn't without one more surprise. A few months after her death, my mother and aunt got a phone call to say Mary Kelly had left them a small sum of money in her will – a token of gratitude for their loyal custom. While we may call it progress to shop in multi-national stores and online supermarkets now, generations of Irish families are indebted to shopkeepers like Mary Kelly.

Swimming Pool Adventure

In 1970 the outdoor swimming pool was opened in Carlow Town Park to the delight of local children and swimming enthusiasts. Prior to that, any of those who could swim, and most people couldn't, swam in the river Barrow. The more serious swimmers were members of the Swimming Club on the Barrow Track where there were modest changing facilities, while families with small children swam at the back of Knockbeg College or at Milford weir where the water was shallow.

But now there was an actual swimming pool – in fact two pools – a thirty-three-metre pool with shallow and deep ends, and a learners' pool, which was always known as the 'baby pool.' With its aquamarine mosaic tiling and spacious dressing rooms, the new pool brought a touch of the exotic to a grey, rural town and became the focus of teenage life in the 1970s.

I was a reluctant swimmer – afraid to take my feet off the ground in case the water swallowed me up. Until I finally learned to swim, aged 11, I regularly sported yellow arm-bands or 'water wings' as we used to call them. With our flowery swimming hats and one-pieces, my sister and I were not exactly in vogue fashion-wise, but it didn't matter. Just being in the water amongst the excited Carlow youth was enough. It was absolutely the place to be.

A trip to the pool was about much more than the one-hour session your 50p could buy you. We'd leave our house with rolled up towels under our arms, call for our friend next door, and set out on our daily adventure. Reaching the Dublin Road, we had a decision to make. Would we walk around by the Courthouse or go 'through the Mental.' In those politically incorrect days, that was what we called St. Dympna's Psychiatric Hospital whose seven-acre manicured grounds had a tree-lined short-cut that took five minutes off our journey.

The fear around people with mental illness at that time outweighed any danger the sad, slow-walking patients actually posed. Mostly they sat on benches outside the hospital building and paid no attention to the passers-by. Others were happily engaged in gardening, maintaining the beautiful flower beds and box-hedges that spelled out 'St. Dympna's Hospital' in large leafy letters.

The dark canopy over the tree-lined path added to the sense of danger as we made our way behind the stone grotto of St. Bernadette kneeling at the feet of the Blessed Virgin Mary of Lourdes. One day we decided to climb it, and all three of us made it to a ledge that was about five feet above the ground. Suddenly we saw the gardener coming, striding across the lawn directly towards us. My friend and I managed to scramble down and were about to run away, but my sister was stuck. We pleaded with her to jump, but it was too late. The big, burly man lifted her down, saying he would tell our parents what we were doing – a threat he didn't carry out, but we felt obliged to confess just in case.

The next part of the journey took us down Grave Lane and into the Town Park. The high slide, swing-boat and roundabout were in constant motion and we looked at them longingly, knowing we'd partake in that exhilarating fun as soon as our swim was over. Then we'd stand in line, waiting for the big gate to be opened, leaving 50p on the counter before racing around the pool to see who'd be first into the water. The weather was irrelevant. In fact, we loved being in the pool in the rain. I even remember staying in the water for a thunderstorm, oblivious to any danger that might have posed.

Then, with wet hair and sticky clothes, we'd emerge to spin each other on the roundabout, take turns pushing the swing-boat that held up to ten children, and run up the twenty-foot slide when we got bored sliding down it. Of course, we had heard about the boy who fractured his skull falling off the swing-boat and the girl who broke her leg on the roundabout. We were all shocked to hear of the fourteen-year-old boy from Cork who drowned in the swimming pool while swimming with his cousins. But, with the optimism of youth, we just assumed nothing bad would happen to us.

Finally, when our time in the playground was up and we were expected home for tea, we had one final call to make. At the end of Grave Lane, 'Nurse Lawlor,' a retired nurse, ran a small sweet shop. The door was rarely open, she mostly preferred to serve her young customers through an open sash window. Sometimes you'd have to wait for a while if she was out the back feeding her ducks and chickens and then, without washing her hands, she'd hand out gobstoppers, 'Scotty dogs' made of jelly and 'Patsy Pops' to sustain us on the way home. Then, tired and happy, we'd hang our togs on the line and prepare to do it all again tomorrow.

Tomboys

When my friend and I were nine or ten, we were tomboys. We never referred to ourselves as such, in fact people who called us that to our faces generally meant to put us down. It was a bit like saying, 'You're not a proper girl,' or, 'You're pretending to be a boy.' But actually it was neither of those things. For us, being tomboys didn't mean we wanted to copy boys or be boys, we wanted to have the same kind of fun as them. We wanted to compete and sometimes win. Deep down we knew that anything a boy could do we could probably do every bit as good, or even better.

Our heroine in those 'Famous Five' days was George, the girl who could outshine her comrades, Julian, Dick and Anne without effort. While her real name was Georgina, she wouldn't answer anyone who addressed her as that. She loved climbing and sailing and was contemptuous of her doll-loving cousin, Anne. We had no time for Anne at all. She was the kind of girl we absolutely didn't want to be – domesticated, helpless, a scaredy-cat. In Enid Blyton's *Five go off in a Caravan* her own brother described her as a 'very good little housekeeper!' That was the last straw!

Jo March in *Little Women* was another inspiring character in children's literature. In an old-fashioned strait-laced world she was feisty and boisterous, with a temper and a sharp tongue. She whistled, which was totally unheard of for a young lady at the time, and that was music to my ears. My friend and I lived next door to each other and, since we were obliged to go home for our meals, we had to come up with a system of letting each other know when we were ready to go out again. We saw some boys doing a low whistle by clasping their hands tightly together and blowing through their thumbs. It took a lot of practice, and I blame it for some of the wrinkles that have developed around my mouth over the years, but we mastered it. And that low whistle, which we could eventually modulate by raising and lowering fingers, became our calling card.

Jodie Foster and Tatum O'Neill were our on-screen heroines. We only had one TV channel, RTE, at the time, but when Jodie featured in the series *Paper Moon* we were hooked. Here was a sassy American girl, smart, brave and tough. Our kind of girl! She was the antithesis to the good convent girls we were being reared to be, and we loved it. And yet, there was nothing bad or devious about her. She just said it like it was. No nonsense and definitely no apology for being a girl.

Tatum O'Neill was in films like *The Bad News Bears* and *Freaky Friday* in the '70's. Sitting in the darkness of the Coliseum cinema in Carlow we imagined we could be that baseball playing, confident kid, who boys looked up to because she was the best, and she knew it. The world of child stars was only opening up for us, and while most conformed to stereotype, the ones who didn't were the most memorable for me. There was more than one way to be a girl. Who knew?

Laura Ingalls and the *Little House on the Prairie* came on the scene a little later. It was a bit saccharin and the girls wore ridiculous dresses by our standards. But Laura, despite her attire, was definitely one of us! She was a plucky girl with spirit and determination. She loved fishing and baseball and, as we watched her grow up, we saw how a spirited young girl could grow into a strong woman, even in a man's world like Walnut Grove, and we were impressed.

In our everyday lives we grew up in a newish housing estate where there were droves of children, all roughly the same age. We passed the summer and the long evenings playing on the greens, building grass-forts, kicking football and playing rounders. We were usually the only girls and the last to be picked for teams. That is, until they got to know us. When they realised that we had more to prove and were willing to give one hundred and ten per cent, we were in.

We learned the hard way that boys don't like being beaten at marbles. Especially by girls. Having gone out on the street with a small bag of plain marbles, some 'Colouredies' which had two tones in the glass, and 'Jarrows' which were the big ones, my friend and I as a deadly duo came home once with twice as many as we started out with. Then, mysteriously, the boys were unavailable to play, and we were left to play kerb-ball on our own for a while until egos had recovered.

I've never been sorry that I spent my childhood climbing trees, crawling through long grass and flying kites. I remember long days full of adventure, going to bed exhausted and jumping up in the morning to the sound of the low whistle that told me my friend was outside and this tomboy was going to have another fun-filled day.

Dining with the Queen

My maternal grandmother was determined that, if she did nothing else, she would instil good table-manners in her five grandchildren and in this duty she was relentless. The pleasure of savouring our food was superseded by the need to ensure our elbows weren't on the table, that we asked for the salt to be passed rather than reach for it, that the soup bowl was tilted away instead of towards us, and a lot of other rules that made little sense then or now. But they were important to Granny and there was no point arguing.

I'm not sure in what company she expected us to mingle when we grew up, but Granny, having been reared with Victorian manners, seemed to feel that our family alone could save the world from uncivilised behaviour, one dinner table at a time. Sitting at the head of the table, her steely grey eyes missed nothing, and her penetrating gaze was only broken to roll her eyes heavenward at our failures of etiquette.

'Oh, I suppose you'll do that when you go to see the Queen!'

My grandmother, born on the longest day of the year 1900, was a live-in governess to a family in Dun Laoghaire in her early twenties, charged with teaching two young girls etiquette and decorum, as well as the rudiments of the English language. When the two girls went to a boarding school for young ladies, Granny continued her mission in Carlow with her own two daughters and, finally, with us.

'Put your knife and fork together when you've finished. In good establishments that indicates to the staff that you're finished your meal,' she'd say.

And we'd look around our humble kitchen, and there wasn't a maid or butler to be seen.

'Sit back down there, young lady. You didn't ask to leave the table,' she'd say.

'May I leave the table please, Granny?'

This was 1974, not 1874, and asking to leave the table got quite a hearty laugh when I tried it in my friend's house.

It was bad manners to eat one pea at a time. There had to be more than one on the fork and the fork could not be used like a shovel. Oh no. That was a definite sign of not knowing what was what. 'Don't talk with your mouth full. Don't slurp when you drink. Keep your elbows in. Don't eat too much or too little. Never wipe your nose or your face with your napkin – only your mouth and chin.'

For a long time, I actually thought that Granny would some day bring me to see the Queen. It seemed like my destiny, since we were always rehearsing for it. I imagined the scene – Granny and I striding up to the big black gates and flashing a gilt-edged invitation to a guard with a bearskin hat. Then the Queen would sit at one end of a long table, ten-year-old me at the other, with Granny's watchful eye in between. I would be shielding my eyes from the reflected light of the crown, while the Queen, with her glasses on the end of her nose, studied the position of my elbows as I ate. And I would have to remind myself not to throw scraps to the Corgis at my feet.

Sometimes, lying in my bed at night, I even wondered should I learn to curtsy. But, alas, no. It soon became apparent that this was a fantasy completely of my grandmother's making, and that in fact, far from being well-prepared for a future of fine dining, we were ill-prepared for the world of Chinese takeaways and drive-thru's that were finger-licking good.

I only remember dining out with Granny once. We were having new Lino laid in the kitchen and the whole family met for lunch in one of the only hotels in Carlow at the time – appropriately for Granny, it was called the Royal Hotel. Not a sign of the Queen though! But it gave me my first chance to exhibit exquisite table manners and Sr. Áine was mightily impressed when I got back to school at 2pm and announced that our family had dined at the Royal.

It's comforting to know that my grandmother, who went to her heavenly reward many years ago, has now been joined by Queen Elizabeth herself. Finally, they might actually get to meet and to share a heavenly repast. I'm sure the Queen will be impressed at my grandmother's impeccable table-manners.

Back in Carlow I often imagine Granny looking down and approving of my efforts on a good day and I hope she doesn't find too much cause to purse her lips and shake her head. I know that on a daily basis she would despair at the sight of her descendants eating from pizza boxes and styrofoam containers. But on the special days, I hope we do her proud. And, although I never got to meet the Queen, she indirectly taught me quite a lot and for that I'm eternally grateful.

Half a Declension!

I was almost a qualified teacher before I understood what a declension was. And sometimes, I'm still not entirely sure. Yet it's over forty years since poor Sr. Agnes, with her earnest face and furrowed brow, did her utmost to explain it to me in a roomful of disinterested 'Honours Irish' girls. I wasn't the only one struggling – a quick glance around the room revealed many a raised eyebrow. Our plight was complicated by the fact that Sister Agnes insisted on explaining the 'Chéad Diochlaonadh' and 'Dara Diochlaonadh' through incomprehensible, grammatical Irish, which only served to confuse us more. There may have been a 'Tríú Diochlaonadh' too, but I was fast asleep by the time she got to that.

I was pretty good at Gaeilge in school. Well, writing it anyway. Speaking it wasn't encouraged, except for the two weeks prior to the oral exam, when, for some reason Sr. Agnes was amazed that we couldn't just turn it on, like a tap. 'Bí ag caint!' she'd exclaim, but our heads were so full of grammar rules and pitfalls, we had never learned to actually communicate. Who knew that was even possible, except for the handful of girls who had been to the Gaeltacht? And we thought they were just 'good at Irish,' while we were just scrabbling around trying to figure out what a declension was.

However, something interesting happened in Irish class once. I got a migraine. Not one of the head-thumping, painful ones – just an aura, like everything was half-there and half-missing. I looked down at the page and the half-words made as little sense as the full ones, but Sr. Agnes's face was

195

intriguing. I could see one half of her nose and her right eye. Where the rest of her should be, was like radiant sunlight and when she moved, I could see a kind of streak of light following her. Looking around, everyone else seemed to be leaning on their hands, doodling, waiting for the class to be over, but I was enthralled. I said, 'Ní thuigim, a shúir,' just to see what it would be like if she looked directly at me. I still didn't understand, but watching half her mouth moving was fascinating.

For the remainder of the class, I was energised. Half-words, half a door, half a nun – Irish was never so interesting. I followed Sister Agnes's streak of light moving like a comet around the ardán, and she clearly noted my new-found enthusiasm, asking me lots of questions, some of which I even knew the answers to. When I floundered she said, in a frustrated voice, 'Féach sa leabhar - tá sé soiléir!' But in my half-world, nothing was soiléir and, finally, she gave up on me and moved on to someone else.

Poor Sister Agnes – we were really cruel to her. Reading from her small purple grammar book, which was her Bible, she spouted about briathra neamhrialta, an chéad réimniù agus an dara réimniú. Séimhiú's, urú's, firinscneach, baininscneach, you name it, Sister Agnes taught it, and by and large we eventually mastered it, but not without causing her lots of heartache. As for the declensions? They remained an elusive dream – an aisling – a spéirbhean – that existed only in Sister Agnes's head!

So, after all these years, I decided to do a little research into what a declension actually is and here's what I found: it actually has two meanings. I'm pretty sure Sr. Mary was referring to the first one, which, in linguistics, means the changing of the form of a word to express its syntactic function in a sentence. God bless her optimism! We didn't know how to say where we lived and what our hobbies were 'as Gaeilge' and yet three days a week we were linguistic scholars. The second meaning is much more interesting.

Apparently, the word declension is also related to the word 'decline.' In archaic English it meant a condition of decline or moral deterioration. Imagine if that's what Sr. Agnes was actually talking about! If only we'd known! We could have attached a whole new meaning to the genitive case that would have made Irish class so much more interesting.

I wonder do many of those girls who sat beside me all those years ago ever think about a declension? When they're on holidays in Spain or France, and they hear the waiter slipping seamlessly from English to Spanish or whatever language is needed, do they wonder, like I do, why we didn't just learn to speak first and leave the academics till later? Would they actually return the mussels and chilled wine if the waiter used the wrong form of the verb? I think not. So many people from other countries have made their home in Ireland and every day they communicate with us through imperfect English. Hey, our own version of English is often not so hot! Who cares? In my opinion, if you want to stop someone trying to communicate in a language that's not their own, tell them about declensions.

But, just in case you think I'm promoting sloppiness in language expression, I'm certainly not. It's just that the words cart and horse come to mind when you put grammar before communication. Language acquisition comes naturally in the right order – you hear it, you assimilate it, you use it and use it and use it. Finally, you learn the subtleties, because you realise you need them to communicate better. Like riding a bike with no stabilisers. Generations in this country have failed to achieve what our European neighbours take for granted – communication is easy. Grammar is a necessary evil. Declensions give you a migraine.

The Fisherman's Cap

I'm not sure exactly when my father started to wear a fisherman's cap, but I think he was well into his fifties. It coincided with his hair-loss having reached a stage that a comb-over couldn't be trusted in a strong wind. It was also around the time of the rise in popularity of the Clancy Brothers and Tommy Makem. Liam Clancy wore a similar type cap, with a small visor and a full, soft crown, rope detail on the front, secured by two covered buttons. Dad eventually amassed quite a selection of these caps, mostly made of corduroy, but he also had some made of denim or navy blue felt. Complete with his well-trimmed beard, he was our very own Captain Birdseye.

Despite his convincing attire, however, Dad was no sailor. His sea-legs were known to let him down in a matter of minutes after the B and I ferry left Dun Laoghaire pier on a voyage to England, and he would have to take to his cabin for the rest of the journey across the Irish Sea. On the longer trips from Rosslare to Cherbourg, he was invariably sick. On these occasions he was happy to let someone else navigate, while he attempted to sleep, leaving strict instructions that no one was to waken him until the boat had docked.

Once, while visiting Athlone for a drama festival, Dad hired a rowing boat for a leisurely afternoon on Lough Ree. There is a photo of him posing, oars in hand, fisherman's cap in place, looking every bit the accomplished sailor. But that was before the storm blew up. A half an hour into the excursion, the weather took a violent turn. The sky darkened and, before he knew it, he was in the eye of the storm. Afterwards he told the story of how he feared for his life when a perfectly calm lake erupted into turbulent waves as a heavy mist descended, and it took him two hours to get back, battling the wind and current all the way.

There are photos of all Dad's grandchildren wearing one of his fisherman's caps. From tiny heads engulfed in blue corduroy to toddlers peering out with one eye covered, Dad's hat was a popular prop. As they got older, if they were ever bored, he'd say, 'Hold out your arm. Now make a fist and hold it up slightly.' Then he'd toss the hat across the room trying to land it directly on the closed fist and accuse them of moving if he missed. Then they would do the same and this time, he would deliberately move, so that the hat fell on the floor to wails of, 'Oh Grandad. That's not fair. You moved!'

When cancer struck and the treatment stole every last rib of hair from his head and face, the fisherman's cap was more important than ever. It made his otherwise bloated face recognisable and helped put the swagger back in his step. It's impossible to quantify the confidence that cap gave him. He was himself again, at least on the outside, the captain of his own ship, and he could navigate the choppy waters of life with his own personal flair.

On what turned out to be one of his final days, the ambulance arrived to bring him home. Wearing his paisley dressing gown and slippers, his diminished frame appeared in the doorway. Knowing he wouldn't want any fuss, we hovered around the gate to see how he was, but we needn't have worried. The ambulance attendant settled him into the wheelchair ready for off, but Dad pointed to something and the door closed over again. Next thing they both emerged, Dad with his fisherman's cap on, and just in case any neighbours were watching, he was waving and smiling like a celebrity.

When he passed away, Dad was laid out in a wicker coffin, as he had requested. It looked like something baby Moses would have floated down the Nile in, although I can't imagine Dad would have enjoyed that journey much.

He was wearing his best suit with a matching handkerchief chosen by my mother, carefully arranged in his pocket. His beard had grown back and was carefully trimmed, and his remaining hair combed to perfection. But there was something missing. 'He doesn't look like himself without the cap,' somebody remarked. A quick scan through his collection on the back of the 'under the stairs' cupboard door yielded the perfect accessory for his final voyage. He was ready for off, equipped with everything he needed. The captain was back at the wheel.

About the author

After a career in teaching spanning thirty years, Maria O'Rourke is now a dedicated writer, having completed a Masters in Creative Writing at the University of Limerick in Ireland.

She draws on her own experiences in personal, work and family life to bring out what is universal in each individual experience. Defying the Curse is her debut novel.

She has recently been awarded the Wild Atlantic Writing Award as well as being shortlisted for the Anthology Short Fiction Competition, the Farnham Flash Fiction Competition and the Liberties Press Humorous Short Story Competition. She has been published by The Blue Nib, The Ogham Stone and The Galway Review. Her story entitled 'Mary Kelly's Shop' has featured on Sunday Miscellany on RTE Radio. Mother to three grown-up children, she lives in Carlow town with her husband, David.

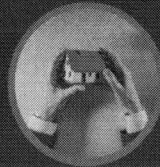

Printed in Great Britain
by Amazon

1ab96096-10e5-4d43-be45-c3ffb422d4beR01